THE BOOK OF RULES
OF TYCONIUS

Its Purpose and Inner Logic

PAMELA BRIGHT

UNIVERSITY OF NOTRE DAME PRESS
Notre Dame, Indiana

Library of Congress Cataloging-in-Publication Data

Bright, Pamela
    The Book of rules of Tyconius.

    (Christianity and Judaism in antiquity; v.2)
    Includes bibliographical references and indexes.
    1. Tyconius, 4th cent. Liber regularum. 2. Bible—
Hermeneutics. 3. Bible—Prophecies. 4. Typology
(Theology) I. Title. II. Series.
BS476.B64 1988   220.6'01   88-40320
ISBN 0-268-01287-3

Manufactured in the United States of America

The Book of Rules
of Tyconius

Christianity and Judaism in Antiquity

CHARLES KANNENGIESSER, SERIES EDITOR

Volume 2

CONTENTS

To my mother and father, Walter and Phyllis Bright

ACKNOWLEDGEMENTS

The present study is a rewriting of the doctoral dissertation, *Liber Regularum Tyconii: A Study of the Hermeneutical Theory of Tyconius, Theologian and Exegete of the North African Tradition,* presented in 1987 at the University of Notre Dame, Indiana. I wish to express my gratitude to Dr. Charles Kannengiesser, S.J. who suggested the *Book of Rules* as a dissertation topic, who guided the research through all its stages, and whose dedication as scholar and teacher has been a constant source of inspiration.

I wish also to thank my readers, Dr. John Collins, Dr. Jean Laporte and Dr. Eugene Ulrich for their encouragement and their suggestions in helping to clarify the lines of argument. To Colleen Smith I wish to express a special word of thanks for her generosity and care in the typing of the manuscript.

I am grateful for the enthusiasm and the professionalism of the staff at the Center for Instructional Design of Loyola University of Chicago without whose assistance this publication would not have been possible.

Pamela Bright
Loyola University of Chicago
May 24, 1988

INTRODUCTION

Just over a hundred years ago, the English scholar F.C. Burkitt was looking for a pre-Augustinian African writer whose citation from the Prophets might shed light on the Old Latin versions of the Bible. He found such a writer in the fourth century Donatist theologian and exegete, Tyconius. The *Liber Regularum* (LR)[1] of Tyconius, a treatise on the interpretation of Scripture, provided Burkitt with a mine of prophetic material for the study of pre-Vulgate Latin Scriptures. Indeed Burkitt claimed that it was "the only considerable body of evidence for the Latin text of the Prophets current in Africa between the epochs of Cyprian and Augustine."[2]

Burkitt recognized that the immediate problem in the study of Tyconius' *Book of Rules* was the state of the printed text which had been first published in the sixteenth century by Grynaeus of Basle.[3]

It is I believe mainly this corrupt state of the text which has prevented the recognition of the very important place which Tyconius holds in the history of Biblical Interpretation in Western Europe.[4]

---

[1]*Liber Regularum* (LR) F. C. Burkitt, *The Book Of Rules of Tyconius* (Cambridge: University Press, 1894, reprint 1967).

[2]Burkitt, *Book of Rules,* Preface.

[3]Burkitt, *Book of Rules,* xxviii.

[4]Burkitt, *Book of Rules,* Preface.

Burkitt published his critical edition of the *Book of Rules* in 1894 but as his attention remained focused on textual criticism rather than upon biblical interpretation, a critical study of the *Book of Rules* as a work of exegetical theory was left to later scholarship. A century after Burkitt's edition was published this intriguing work still awaits adequate research. The present study is indicative of the growing awareness of the place of this African theologian in the history of Christian exegesis. The basic premise of the research is that Tyconius must first be studied directly from his own works rather than indirectly through the many commentators of the ancient and medieval Church who have been influenced by his ideas.

Tyconius was one of the most incisive thinkers of the African Church in the seventies and eighties of the fourth century. From his pen came the commentary on the Apocalypse that influenced exegetes for the next millennium. A second work, the *Book of Rules*, was the first treatise on biblical hermeneutics in the Latin West. Both works have had a checkered history. The Apocalypse commentary has been lost, and its remains lie scattered, either as source or as influence, in the works of medieval exegetes, thus providing a major task of literary reconstruction for the modern scholar.[5]

The *Book of Rules* has remained intact. It has suffered a different fate. Tyconius' fame as a thinker and writer extended beyond the Donatist community, but his star was eclipsed by that of Augustine, whose return to Africa in 388 renewed the fortunes of the Catholic party. Augustine was intrigued by the thought of the Donatist author, and summarized the seven rules of Tyconius in the *De Doctrina Christiana*.[6] The prestige of Augustine's

---

[5]K. Steinhauser, *The Apocalypse Commentary of Tyconius: A History of Its Reception and Influence* (Frankfurt: Peter Lang, 1987).

[6]Augustine, *De Doctrina Christiana* III, 30-37, PL 34:16-121.

summary effectively deflected attention from Tyconius' text, a decisive factor in the history of the *Book of Rules*.

The aim of the present work is to return to the text of the *Book of Rules*, and to provide an introduction to a book that needs to be read in its entirety for a just appreciation of a work so stamped with the mind of its author – at once original, creative and rigorously systematic. It is an introduction in the sense of a "re-introduction" to an acknowledged classic among the works of biblical interpretation of the past, but which has only recently been translated into a modern language. It is also a "re-introduction" to a work that has suffered serious distortion in the series of paraphrased or summarized versions through which it has been known even when the most influential of these comes from Augustine himself.[7]

In a more technical sense, the study is intended as an introduction to the purpose and inner logic of the *Book of Rules*. It examines the author's criteria for the selection of biblical texts. It seeks to understand both the "logic" of the seven rules and the logic of the author's structuring of the book as a whole. How does this literary structure throw light on the hermeneutical theory that underlies Tyconius' description of the seven "mystical rules" of Scripture?

It is now close to a century since Burkitt published his critical edition of the *Book of Rules*, but at the very time that Burkitt provided this access to the work of Tyconius, the whole understanding of the nature and purpose of scriptural exegesis was on the point of being revolutionized. In his preface, Burkitt argued for the need of a contemporary reappraisal of Tyconius'

---

[7]P. Bright, "Tyconius and His Interpreters," C. Kannengiesser, *A Conflict of Christian Hermeneutics in Roman Africa: Tyconius vs. Augustine* (Center for Hermeneutical Studies. Berkeley, Ca. Forthcoming, 1989).

interpretative methodology, but to respond to such a challenge today is to address at best a limited and specialized readership. To be invited into a world where terms like "spiritual interpretation," "typology," let alone the infamous "allegory," are given respectful consideration is like entering a time warp. The tools and methodology of modern biblical criticism have so transformed the mental landscape that the presuppositions and the methodologies of the exegetes of the early centuries of the Church seem like those of alien life-forms.

Like great scarred monuments of the past, the vast biblical commentaries of the early Church, the hermeneutical works extolling the importance of the "spiritual senses" of Scripture, and the theological treatises studded with "proof-texts" seem part of a revered but irrevocably remote past. They gather dust on library shelves, or if taken down can only be regarded as source material for patristic or medieval scholarship. It is not that these works are devoid of charm or of spiritual insight – witness Augustine's Commentaries on 1 John[8] – but it is precisely the revolutionary changes in biblical hermeneutics in our own century that make much of the writings of the early Church impenetrable to the modern reader.

To remove some of the barriers to a renewed appreciation of a vast literature of the Christian past calls for a reconsideration of the hermeneutics of the early Church; but this in itself can seem an arduous and rather fruitless task in the face of the more immediate and urgent challenges posed to the modern theologian by the rapidity of cultural change today. In Macbeth's phrase, "returning were as tedious as go o'er."[9]

---

[8] Augustine, "On the First Epistle of John: Sermon X," *Early Christian Spirituality*, ed. C. Kannengiesser, trans. P. Bright (Sources of Early Christian Thought; Philadephia: Fortress Press, 1986) 101-113.

[9] *Macbeth*, act 3, sc 4.

In spite of these reservations, the need of a reappraisal of the hermeneutics of the early Church has been championed by a number of scholars over the past thirty or forty years, notably by the French scholars, Henri de Lubac and Jean Daniélou. In a 1950 issue of *Theological Studies*, Walter Burghardt referred to the study of early Christian exegesis as "one of the liveliest issues in contemporary theological discussion":

> The bulk of significant contributions stems from French and Belgian pens, the shock of the controversy is felt most keenly by Alexandrian exegetes, notably Clement and Origen; the field of discussion is the doctrine of scriptural senses; and in practice the point of heaviest concentration is patristic theory and practice of the so-called spiritual sense of Scripture - the typology or allegorism of Christian antiquity.[10]

Burghardt judged that the ultimate frame of reference was much broader than the question of whether the modern exegete is aware of the subtlety and the variety of the understandings of what was meant by the spiritual sense of Scripture among the early exegetes.

> The cataclysmic events of a decade and more have served to sharpen in many minds the lingering suspicion of a cleavage between Christian thought and Christian life, between theology and spirituality. The realization has had its repercussion in several fields of research, more obviously perhaps in the intensification of the liturgical renaissance, in the movement towards a more vital contact

---

[10]W. J. Burghardt, "On Early Christian Exegesis," *Theological Studies* 11 (1950) 78.

with patristic thought, and in an effort to explore and exploit the possibilities inherent in a more profound penetration of the bonds that link the Old Testament with the New.[11]

With doggedness, with flashes of luminous insight, with frequent recriminations among themselves,[12] a small army of scholars set to work on the texts of Clement, Origen, Augustine, the Syriac sources, in fact across the wide scope of patristic exegesis. For all the enthusiasm and scholarly finesse of the investigation, many other scholars of the nineteen forties and fifties remained unconvinced of the value of their efforts.

> One sees why it is impossible to consider the patristic exegesis as a treasure from which we have only to draw in all confidence, or even as an example to be followed. The Fathers have penetrated deeply into the religious teaching of Scripture; they are a wonderful help for us to do the same in our turn. But in their techniques for cultivating the sacred text there have been too many divergences among them, too much excess in some of them, for us to be able to think that they have given a definitive solution to the difficult problem of the spiritual sense. They can doubtless awaken our attention, arouse our interest for an investigation which the modern study of the Bible could make [us] slight and even regard as definitely outdated. We will learn from their efforts and their discussions, but for a principle of discrimination we shall have to look elsewhere.[13]

---

[11]Burghardt, "On Early Christian Exegesis," 78.

[12]Burghardt, "On Early Christian Exegesis," 116.

[13]Burghardt, "On Early Christian Exegesis," 115.

Why then a study of the hermeneutical theory of Tyconius whose *Book of Rules* proposes not one but *seven* "principles of discrimination"? And why of all people a man like Tyconius, marginalized as he was in his own lifetime? Here is a lay theologian in the age of theologian-bishops like Athanasius, Hilary, and Ambrose. Here is a member of a schismatic Church, out of favor with his own Donatist bishop, Parmenian, the forceful and intelligent successor of Donatus the Great in the see of Carthage. Tyconius is hardly a prolific author. He is known to have written four books,[14] but his reputation rests upon the two books that survived him, a commentary on the Apocalypse, now lost, and the *Book of Rules*, the subject of this study. The *Book of Rules* was recommended by a long line of theologians beginning with Augustine, the younger contemporary of Tyconius. With such a commendation it is no wonder that the *Book of Rules* found its way into Catholic readership, that it was diligently copied by later generations of monks, and that it was summarized and listed in catalogues of exegetical works for over a thousand years; but was it *read*, at least read in its entirety? It will be argued in this study that the *Book of Rules* has suffered the fate of many another classic work, in being praised rather than read. Perhaps one could ask, even if it has been read, has it been read without certain subtle prejudices or read in a fragmentary fashion that does not appreciate the systematic unity of the whole?

In spite of the negatives which loom large in such a study both from the point of view of the history of the *Book of Rules* itself and of the broader question of the value of the study of patristic exegesis, this ancient author

---

[14]Gennadius, *De Viris inlustribus* 18 ed. Richardson (Texte und Untersuchungen 14. The Nicene and Post-Nicene Fathers, second series 3, ed. P. Schaf, H. Wace; Grand Rapids, MI: Wm. Eerdmans, 1952) 285-402.

presents us with a profoundly modern challenge. What have the ancient writings of Israel to say to the Christian Church? Where Tertullian, insisting upon the superiority of Scripture over philosophy, asks what has Athens to do with Jerusalem, Tyconius, his fellow African, asks perhaps a more pene-trating question – what have ancient Tyre, pharaonic Egypt and the long van-ished Assyria to do with the Christian Churches of Africa in the fourth century?

It is another form of the question that Marcion asked the Christian Church in the second century – what *are* the Scriptures of the Church? In our own century in the wake of fundamental shifts in exegesis the question of the reception of Scripture in the Church has become pivotal. In what sense can the Hebrew Scriptures be a source for theology and spiritual life for the Christian Church without denying the profound changes in exegetical theory in modernity?

Throughout the *Book of Rules*, Tyconius concentrates on the ques-tion of the relevance of prophetic texts for the Christian Church. It is not so much a question of the fulfillment or non-fulfillment in the past or in some eschatological future – but what does prophecy mean for Africa in the closing years of the fourth century? What can it mean for Africa, for whom the cities and kings against which the prophets thundered were as remote as they are for us today? Why should Tyconius' fellow Africans care about prophecies against the long-dead Prince of Tyre (Ezek 28:2-19) and the King of Babylon (Isa 14:12-21) when the Donatist community was facing the repressions of the Count Romanus and the Proconsul Hesperius under orders of a Christian Emperor?[15]

---

[15]W. H. C. Frend, *The Donatist Church* (Oxford: Clarendon Press, 1952) 203. The Donatist Church suffered repressions under Count Romanus in 364, and under Proconsul Herperius in 376.

The purpose of Tyconius' work, as he states in the preamble to the *Book of Rules*, is to provide a guide through the "immense forest of prophecy," but Tyconius does not restrict the term "prophecy" to the oracles of the prophets of Israel. One of the most urgent questions for both the study of the *Book of Rules* and for the fragments of the *Apocalypse Commentary* is to define what "prophecy" meant for Tyconius. The analysis of the criteria for the selection of scriptural texts in the *Book of Rules* in Chapter Two of the present work reveals that although Tyconius includes a very great number of texts from the books of the Prophets that speak words of encouragement or of admonition, there is just as much emphasis upon threats and promises from the New Testament authors. From a study of the texts Tyconius selects for comment, it becomes evident that for Tyconius a "prophetic" text is one that calls sinners to repentance by warning of the death and destruction that awaits those that are separated from the love of God.

This concentration of texts from both the Old and the New Testament upon the consequences of sin makes a first reading of the *Book of Rules* a somewhat somber experience. The final words of the book are a stark description of the annihilation awaiting the members of the Church who have become separated from Christ: "You are destined for destruction" (Ezek 28:19). Tyconius' purpose is far from negative. He opposed the fundamental ecclesiology of the Donatist Church when he insisted that the Church was not the holy remnant of the End Times waiting for its vindication in the glory of the Second Coming. It was a mixed society still graced with the word of God calling the sinner to repentance.

Tyconius was the first African to use the term "spiritual" interpretation of Scripture. What he meant by spiritual interpretation was that the Spirit, the Author of Scripture, reveals present *spiritual* realities rather than the shape of future eschatological events. Tyconius' fellow

Donatists were indeed suffering persecution at the hands of fellow Christians, one of the signs of the "End Times," but the revelation of the Spirit in Scripture is not about the destruction that awaits those persecutors roused up by the Antichrist. Tyconius argues that the knowledge that the ultimate victory of Christ over the Antichrist in the "end times" is hardly a mystery to be wrested from the text by exegesis. The prophetic denunciations speak of "spiritual" death and destruction that is already present in the Church. Tyconius claims that Scripture speaks of the present reality of sin – the "mystery of evil" at work in the Church – rather than of the cataclysms of the end times which will be visible to all.

When Tyconius speaks of present "spiritual" realities – the invisible growth and spread of evil throughout the Church, he does not repeat the Gnostic devaluation of time and material reality. For a man of his time Tyconius had a keen sense of history.

> A system of interpretation which frankly recognizes the historical meaning of prophecy without thereby detracting from its spiritual essence should have some interest in the present day.[16]

He is aware of the distance between himself and the cities of the past that had been denounced by the Prophets. In tune with the traditional eschatological awareness of the African Church, Tyconius expects the Second Coming of Christ, but the Second Coming is such a matter of the common faith of the Church that it needs neither emphasis nor argument, but it is not yet! These are not yet the days of the manifest glory of Christ. The prophecies of the Second Coming cited with such frequency throughout the *Book of Rules* are still sealed. They are not yet visible to all. In the preamble to the

---

[16]Burkitt, *Book of Rules,* Preface.

Book of Rules, Tyconius claims that the "treasures" of Scripture are invisible "to some" (LR 1:5). The seven "mystical rules" themselves hide the "treasures" so that they are "closed," only to be opened by the Spirit; they are "obscure," only to be "illumined" (LR 1:7) by the Spirit. The "breaking open" of these sealed mysteries reveals that the "coming" of the Antichrist is a present *invisible* reality within the Church. This is the revelation to the Church concerning the "man of sin" (2 Thess 2:7).

Both the glory of the Church and the "mystery of evil" are still hidden, invisible, that is, "spiritual" realities. In this sense, Tyconius can call the Church a "spiritual world" where the saving work of God is an on-going reality. It is to this "spiritual world," the Church, that the Spirit addresses exhortations. Though anchored in the past, and directed toward the future, Scripture reveals the *present* choice between good and evil for each individual. It is not for the "signs of the end times" that one scrutinizes the Scriptures – but rather for the signs of what makes one united or separated from Christ now. This separation, now a hidden, "spiritual" reality, is what will be manifest to all at the end-time.

This "spiritual" interpretation of prophecy reveals how far Tyconius deviated from Donatist ecclesiology. He refused the notion of the apostasy of the non-Donatist Christian Churches at the beginning of the Constantinian peace. Even more daringly for a Donatist, he refused to recognize the Donatist Church as the visible faithful remnant waiting the return of the Lord.

Tyconius is remarkable for his refusal of any narrow sectarian view of the Church. Augustine and his fellow Catholics were astonished at the universal vision of the Donatist theologian,[17] but there is no question of

---

[17]Augustine, *De Doctrina Christiana* III, 30.

compromise for the sake of unity in the ecclesiology of the Donatist author. In the *Book of Rules* he claims that the Church is "bipartite," with good and evil membership throughout the world. Augustine had wondered how a man who, in Augustine's terms, "had argued victoriously" against schism in the Church did not choose to join the Catholic party. The answer lies in Tyconius' very understanding of the Church as "bipartite."

> Again, that the Body of Christ is bipartite is shown in this brief sentence: "I am dark and beautiful" (Cant 1:5)... Our text gives an explanation of why she is both dark and beautiful: "like the tent of Kedar, like the leather tent of Solomon" (Cant 1:5). It shows us two tents, the king's and the slave's; yet both are Abraham's off-spring, for Kedar is the son of Ishmael... Nevertheless, we cannot say that the tent of Kedar is outside the Church. Our text speaks of the tent of Kedar and of Solomon, and therefore it says of both: "I am dark " and "I am beautiful." (LR 10:13-30)[18]

The Spirit, through the Scriptures, speaks the word of exhortation and admonition to the Church. The "spiritual" interpretation of the Scripture is a charismatic work, that is, under the grace of the Spirit the prophetic word is addressed to the "bipartite" Church. It is a word of exhortation and encouragement to those on the "right"; it is a word of warning to those of the "left" with the express purpose that the whole Church be re-called to love and unity with Christ, the Head of the Body.

Writing nearly forty years ago, Durbarle had spoken with mixed feelings of the values of patristic exegesis for our times. "We will learn from

---

[18]K. Froehlich, *Biblical Interpretation in the Early Church* (Sources of Early Christian Thought, ed. W. Rusch; Philadelphia: Fortress Press, 1984) 112.

their efforts and their discussions but for a principle of discernment we shall have to look elsewhere . . ."[19] It is true that we can learn much from a fourth-century work such as the *Book of Rules* of Tyconius. We can become more aware of the theological concerns that shaped the exegesis of the early Church, and at the same time we can learn more about the exegetical methods that shaped theology. This is particularly notable in the case of Tyconius where ecclesiology, eschatology and hermeneutical theory are so interrelated.

As Durbarle argued, there is no question of setting the clock back. The point of studying past exegetical methods is to recognize them as belonging to the past. It is not a question of some kind of nostalgic return to a golden age of spiritual interpretation. To study an exegete like Tyconius is to assume the past, rather than to repeat it. More, it is to stand beside a man of the Scriptures, who is at the same time a man of the Church as he probes the reasons why these writings are sacred for him and for his community.

This relationship between Scripture and community remains a fundamental question. It is a question for the scholar in the field of comparative religion. It is a question for the Sunday homilist. It is a question for anyone who reads Scripture today. In pondering this question, it may be argued that in Tyconius, the author of the first treatise on hermeneutics in the Western Church, we are in distinguished company.

---

[19]Burghardt, "On Early Christian Exegesis," 115.

CHAPTER ONE

THE *BOOK OF RULES* – A NEGLECTED CLASSIC

THE LITERARY HISTORY OF THE BOOK OF RULES

In tracing the manuscript tradition of the *Book of Rules*, Burkitt came across a *memoria technica* of the seven rules of Tyconius in a thirteenth century Laon manuscript, first published in the French Departmental Catalogue 5/1849.

Regula prima caput nostrum cum corpore iungit.

corpore de uero loquitur mixtoque secunda.

tertia describit quid lex quid gratia possit.

quarta genus speciem totum partemque rependit.

tempora disiungit maiora minoraque quinta.

sexta refert iterum que primo facta fuerunt.

septima serpentis tibi [1] membra caputque resoluit.

The first rule links our Head with the Body.

The second speaks of the Body, true and mingled.

The third describes what Law and what grace can do.

The fourth decides between genus and species, the whole and the part.

The fifth differentiates greater and lesser times.

---

[1]*Tibi* variant of the Roman mss. Vat 4296 (15th Cent.). *Sibi* 13th cent MS at Laon (Departmental Catalogue of 1849, vol i, 88).

The sixth reports yet again the things which took place originally.

The seventh destroys for you the head and members of the serpent.[2]

There are two Roman manuscript copies of the fourteenth and fifteenth centuries of this deft abridgment of the *Book of Rules*. It should come as no surprise that such an exegetical tool exists since the *Book of Rules* had been part of the standard listings of exegetical works in the Church since the time of Cassiodorus in the sixth century. Isidore of Seville described the Rules in his *Liber Sententiarum* in the seventh century and Bede prefixed his *Explanatio Apocalypsis* with a description of Tyconius' *Book of Rules*. The scholarly Hincmar, in his dispute with Godescalc, referred to Tyconius and his seven rules.

Hincmar, Archbishop of Reims in the second half of the ninth century, has a special place in the literary history of the *Book of Rules* since he gave what Burkitt considers to be "the oldest and best manuscript of it now known"[3] to the Cathedral library at Reims. This vellum quarto Codex Remensis in Carolingian minuscules consists of 35 lines of 139 columns in all. Burkitt has traced the rest of the intact manuscripts of the *Book of Rules*, with one exception, to a single Vatican manuscript of the tenth century, *Codex Vaticanus Reginensis* 590. The exception referred to is a vellum manuscript of the ninth century, *Codex Modoetianus*, "Ambrosiaster's" commentary on the Pauline epistles. The last five pages of the manuscript are an abridgment of the *Book of Rules* known as the Monza Epitome.

---

[2]Burkitt, *Book of Rules*, 86. Memoria Technica for the Rules of Tyconius, from a 13th cent MS at Laon (Departmental Catalogue of 1849, vol i, 88).

[3]Burkitt, *Book of Rules*, xxi.

Burkitt has included a transcript of this document in an appendix to his critical edition of the *Book of Rules*.[4]

Burkitt's study of the literary history of the *Book of Rules* demonstrates how problematic the textual transmission proved for the understanding of Tyconian hermeneutics. When one compares the Vatican codex and Hincmar's copy of the *Book of Rules*, the latter is far superior. Since, according to Burkitt,[5] the Vatican Codex is the ancestor of the remaining witnesses, Codex Parisiensis of the eleventh century and Codex Oxoniensis of the twelfth century, the corruption of the manuscript tradition had an adverse effect upon the reception of Tyconius' exegetical teachings.

THE NEGLECTED CLASSIC

What does it mean to describe the *Book of Rules* as a neglected classic? Burkitt argued that what led to its being neglected and gradually forgotten by the end of the nineteenth century was the poor state of its textual transmission. However, there is another sense in which the *Book of Rules* may be described as neglected. A close study of the references to the *Book of Rules* reveals that Tyconius' work has been read *indirectly* rather than directly from the original. The *Book of Rules* has been read mainly through the eyes of Augustine who included a summary of the seven rules of Tyconius in his own exegetical work, the *De Doctrina Christiana*.

Burkitt sums up the influence of Augustine upon the reception of the *Book of Rules* in the Introduction to the critical edition.

---

[4]Burkitt, *Book of Rules*, 89-98.

[5]Burkitt, *Book of Rules*, xxv.

... the sole reference to Tyconius' book independent of the review in *De Doctrina Christiana* is that by the author of the *de Promissionibus*. He was an African, and perhaps for that reason familiar with the book which his countryman had written less than a century before. Both Cassian and John the Deacon quote the *Book of Rules* only to illustrate a passage where Tyconius' explanation had already been noticed by Augustine. Cassiodorus names Tyconius only in the sentence in which he recommends the study of the *De Doctrina Christiana*; Isidore follows Augustine's remarks more than the original Seven Rules. Therefore, it is not unlikely that the fame of the Book in the middle ages and its preservation to the present day is entirely due to Augustine. It was his recommendation, rather than the intrinsic merit of the work of a Donatist, that secured the respect of Latin Christendom.[6]

It is the "intrinsic merit" of the work of Tyconius that is the subject of the present inquiry. It will be argued that it was precisely the "intrinsic merit" of the *Book of Rules* that was obscured by Augustine. It was obscured not only by the authority of Augustine so that the seven rules were read in Augustine's summarized version rather than in their original form in the *Book of Rules*, but the hermeneutical theory itself was obscured by Augustine's misunderstanding of the fundamental principles of Tyconius' system of exegesis.

The relationship between the two works, the *Liber Regularum* of Tyconius and the *De Doctrina Christiana* of Augustine will be examined more closely in Chapter Five, which investigates the meaning of "rule" in

---

[6]Burkitt, *Book of Rules*, xxiv.

the *Book of Rules*. For the immediate purpose of investigating why the *Book of Rules* has remained an "unread classic" of biblical hermeneutics we turn to the historical context of Augustine's own reading of Tyconius' exegetical treatise.

AUGUSTINE'S SUMMARY OF THE BOOK OF RULES

When Augustine returned to his native Africa in 388, he came as a recent convert to a Church already venerable in its martyrs, a Church with a theological tradition dating back to Tertullian and Cyprian. It was also a Church deeply divided. The unity for which Cyprian had striven in the middle years of the third century had been disrupted by the bitter dispute over the Carthaginian See in the early years of the Constantinian peace.

When Augustine began to share the fruits of his study of Scripture and his methods of scriptural exegesis with his fellow Catholics in the *De Doctrina Christiana*, begun in 396, already more than eighty years had passed since Donatus and his party had refused the validity of the election of Caecilius in 312. Mutual recriminations, individual acts of violence, popular uprisings, imperial repressions, even civil war had ensued. Both parties, Donatist and Catholic, claimed the marks of the true Church, theirs were the enspirited waters of baptism, theirs the true bishop, the true altar. Both sides laid claim to be heir to a hallowed tradition and looked to the vindication of their claims when Christ was to appear in the glory of his Second Coming – soon!

The Scriptures were invoked by both sides. In the disputes between the two bishops, the Donatist Parmenian and the Catholic Optatus of Milevis in the sixties, seventies, and eighties of the fourth century, we can hear echoes of these debates. The Donatists could point to the horror of Christian persecuting Christian as a sign that the last days were upon the earth. Soon the faithful remnant would be sealed for victory (Rev 7:1-8). On the other hand, the Catholic Optatus would argue that the Donatists, in withdrawing from the unity of the Church, had disobeyed the injunction of the lord of the harvest in Matthew's Gospel (Matt 13:29) that there was to be "no separation until the judgment."

While Optatus and Parmenian battled over the interpretation of Scripture in favor of their particular party, Tyconius was also joining the fray, but his strategy involved a more difficult maneuver. His strategy was to open the battle lines on two fronts. On the one side he defended his fellow Donatists as the victims of persecution; on the other he insisted that the Church, the Body of Christ, was to be found throughout the world – certainly beyond the confines of Africa. Augustine expressed his surprise at what Tyconius had written about the catholicity of the Church in the *Book of Rules*:

> A certain Tyconius, who wrote most triumphantly against the Donatists, although he himself was a Donatist and hence is found to have had an absurd mentality where he did not wish to abandon them altogether, wrote a book which he called *of Rules*, since in it he explained seven rules with which, as if with keys, the obscurities of the Divine Scriptures might be opened.[7]

It was more than the ecclesiology of Tyconius that intrigued Augustine and his circle. In a letter to Bishop Aurelius of Carthage in 397, Augustine remarks,

---

[7] Augustine, *On Christian Doctrine* (The Nicene and Post-Nicene Fathers (NPNF), First Series 3, ed. P Schaff, trans. J.F. Shaw; Grand Rapids, MI: Eeardmans, 1956) 568.

On my part I am not forgetting what you asked about the seven rules or keys of Tyconius, and as I have written many times, I am waiting to hear what you think of it.[8]

In the mid 390's, Augustine was drawing up a program for the study and interpretation of Scripture:

There are certain rules for the interpretation of Scripture which I think might with great advantage be taught to earnest students of the Word . . .[9]

Augustine was to draw upon the "gold of Egypt,"[10] his own past secular training, as well as upon traditional Christian exegetical methods in presenting his material. In 396 he broke off his work well into the third book of the *De Doctrina Christiana*. Augustine did not resume this particular work until 427, by concluding the third book and adding a fourth on the style of homiletics. It is in finishing the third book which actually concludes his study of exegetical method in the *De Doctrina Christiana* that Augustine summarizes and comments upon the *Book of Rules* of Tyconius.[11]

It was over thirty years since Augustine had first read Tyconius' treatise on scriptural interpretation. The bishop of Hippo was now a figure of such eminence in the Church that his approbation of a work written nearly

---

[8]Augustine *Letter* 41, *St. Augustine's Letters* vol, 1, trans. W. Parsons (Washington: Catholic University of America Press, 1951) 179.

[9]Augustine, *On Christian Doctrine*, 510.

[10]Augustine, *On Christian Doctrine*, 76.

[11]Augustine, *De Doctrina Christiana* III, 30-37.

half a century before by a Donatist author was decisive for the subsequent history of the *Book of Rules*.[12] Augustine's summary was to prove a fateful vehicle for Tyconius' thought.[13]

Burkitt notes that Augustine's commendation was not without reserve.[14]

> The great African theologian suggests a fresh title for Rules II and III, and gently complains that the treatment of Promises and Law is not quite full enough for the times of the Pelagian controversy. He also warns readers not to forget that Tyconius was not a Catholic: *"Caute sane legendus est, non solum propter quaedam in quibus ut homo errauit, sed maxime propter illa quae sicut Donatista haereticus loquitur."*[15] But this is Augustine's hardest word, and indeed throughout the whole review he treats Tyconius as an authority to be explained rather than as a theorist to be criticized.[16]

Augustine had certainly treated Tyconius as an "authority to be explained," but were his "explanations" to the point? The present work will argue that not only did Augustine misunderstand what Tyconius meant by "the immense forest of prophecy" but that Tyconius and Augustine had diametrically opposed views on key issues in hermeneutics, such as the meaning

---

[12]Burkitt, *Book of Rules,* xviii.

[13]P. Bright, "Tyconius and His Interpreters." The paper concentrates on the comparison of the early summaries of the *Book of Rules*.

[14]Burkitt, *Book of Rules*, xxiii.

[15]Augustine, *De Doctrina Christiana* III, 30.

[16]Burkitt, *Book of Rules,* xviii.

and function of "obscurity" in Scripture as well as the notion of "rule" itself. It is ironic that Augustine's interest in the Donatist's hermeneutical theory effectively blocked its being understood by the wider church community. There is a double irony in this. While Tyconius' exegetical theory may have been misrepresented by Augustine, the fact that the *Book of Rules* itself survived was no doubt due to Augustine's summary in the *De Doctrina Christiana*.

One of the principal aims of this study is to return to the *Book of Rules* itself, to analyze its literary structure and so to establish the relationship between the literary structure and the hermeneutical principles which the author is attempting to explain. When Augustine misunderstands the theory of the *Book of Rules* and ignores its literary structure by truncating the argument and adding new material in his own commentary, there are considerable grounds for arguing that the *Book of Rules* is a neglected classic.

THE BOOK OF RULES IN THE TWENTIETH CENTURY

One of the paradoxes of the study of Tyconius is that while the twentieth century has seen something of a renaissance of Tyconian studies, these studies have not yet focused upon the hermeneutical theory of the *Book of Rules*. Tyconius' work may still be regarded as neglected, at least as an exegetical treatise. There are a number of reasons for this neglect beyond the obvious explanation of Tyconius' theories being judged so removed from the concerns of modern exegesis.

In a sense, the fault lies in the *Book of Rules* itself. The very richness and complexity of Tyconius' thought has tended to distract twentieth-century scholarship from the study of the hermeneutical theory of the *Book of Rules*. In the past century, the main areas of Tyconian research have been in relation to the study of the Old Latin versions of the Bible, Apocalypse

Commentaries, and general questions concerning African Christianity, in particular ecclesiology. Finally, Tyconius has been most commonly studied within the ambiance of Augustinian studies.

Burkitt's research into the Tyconian text of the *Book of Rules*, as well as his study of other citations from the Old Latin versions, convinced him that these Old Latin Scriptures of the African Church were an important witness to the textual history of the Septuagint. Since the discovery of the Qumran texts has stimulated the investigation into the textual history of the Greek texts, the long quotations from the Prophets, particularly from Isaiah, has made for renewed interest in the *Book of Rules* as a source for text criticism.[17]

Scholars in the area of Apocalypse Commentaries have a special interest in the work of Tyconius. While his *Book of Rules* has survived intact, his *Apocalypse Commentary* has been lost. In a recent study of the history of the reception and influence of the work, Kenneth Steinhauser comments on the obstacle to the progress of Tyconian research.

> This loss (of the *Apocalypse Commentary*) not only limits our access to the thought of a controversial churchman and independent theologian but also deprives us of the first attempt in the western church to apply a system of exegetical rules to the interpretation of a single biblical book.[18]

---

[17]Burkitt, *Book of Rules*, vii. See also Burkitt, The *Old Latin and the Itala*. ed. J. Armitage Robinson (Texts and Studies vol.4, 3; Cambridge: University Press, 1896).

[18]Steinhauser, *The Apocalypse Commentary of Tyconius*, 2.

Gennadius, in his survey of ecclesiastical writing at the end of the fifth century, gave special attention to the *Apocalypse Commentary* in his review of the work of Tyconius.[19]   Modern scholarship has affirmed Gennadius' appreciation of the importance of Tyconius' insistence on the "spiritual" interpretation of the text of Revelation.

> . . . he (Tyconius) doubts that there will be a reign of the righteous on the earth for a thousand years after the resurrection, or that there will be two resurrections of the dead in the flesh, one of the righteous and the other of the unrighteous.[20]

Tyconius' rejection of literalistic, millennarian interpretations is pivotal in the Latin tradition of Apocalypse Commentaries. His vigorous insistence on a "spiritual" interpretation of the prophetic texts, rather than the millennarianism of Irenaeus, Tertullian, Hippolytus, and Victorinus of Pettau, turned the tide in the Latin West and made his commentary the most influential of the Apocalypse commentaries in the Western Church.

Jerome used Tyconius' commentary to "correct" the chiliastic interpretations in the late third-century commentary of Victorinus of Pettau, also an African, martyred under Diocletian.   It is one of the tasks of modern scholarship to explore the influence of Tyconius on Augustine's eschatology. In this respect it is interesting to read a footnote in a nineteenth-century translation of Augustine's *City of God:*

> Augustine, who had formerly himself entertained chiliastic hopes, revolutionized the prevailing ante-Nicene view of the Apocalyptic

---

[19]Gennadius, *De Viris Inlustribus,* 18.

[20]Gennadius, *Lives of Illustrious Men,* 389.

millennium by understanding it of the present age of Christ and the church.[21]

It is in this very section of the *City of God* that the influence of Tyconius on the thought of Augustine is most evident. The Augustinian commentator was unaware that Augustine was adopting the "revolutionary" ideas of Tyconius.[22]

A study of the sources for Tyconius' lost *Commentary* was undertaken by J. Haussleiter some years prior to Burkitt's study of the *Book of Rules*.[23] The publication of the "Turin Fragments" of Tyconius' Commentary in 1963 has confirmed the importance of this manuscript in the task of identifying the authentic Tyconian elements in the Apocalypse Commentaries in writers to the ninth century when the monastery of St. Gall still possessed a copy of the Tyconian *Commentary*.[24]

---

[21]Augustine, *The City of God,* trans. M.Dods (NPNF vol.2; Grand Rapids, Mi: Eerdmans, 1956) 426, footnote 5.

[22]Augustine, *The City of God* , Book XX, chapters 5-11, echo the concerns, the arguments, and the scriptural citations of the *Book of Rules* of Tyconius: the "two resurrections," the "thousand years" of the Church. However, in chapter 17 and chapter 19, Augustine takes issue with Tyconius' interpretation of Rev 21, the "heavenly Jerusalem," and with 2 Thess 2, the revelation of the "mystery of iniquity."

[23]J. Haussleiter, "Die lateinische Apokalypse der alten afrikanischen Kirche." *Forschungen zur Geschichte des neutestamenlichen Kanons und der altkirchlichen Literatur.* ed. Theodor Zahn, vol. IV (Erlangen: Deichert, 1891) 1-224.

[24]Francesco Lo Bue, ed., *The Turin Fragments of Tyconius' Commentary on Revelation* (Texts and Studies NS 3; Cambridge: Cambridge University Press, 1963).

Steinhauser's study considers nine authors who had access to the Tyconian *Commentary:*

> Proceeding chronologically, we have Jerome's revision of the Commentary of Victorinus of Pettau, the so-called pseudo-Augustinian homilies written by Caesarius of Arles, the Commentary of Primasius of Hadrumetum, the Complexiones of Cassiodore, the Commemoratorium of pseudo-Jerome, an anonymous capitulary contained in the Codex Oratii B6, the commentary of Bede the Venerable, the lengthy commentary of Ambrosius Autpertus, and finally the commentary of Beatus of Liebana.[25]

The complexity of the task of reconstructing the Tyconian *Commentary* is an added impetus to understanding his thought as it is developed in his *Book of Rules*. The analysis of Tyconius' scriptural citations in the *Book of Rules* in Chapter Two of the present work suggests that there were strong thematic links between the *Book of Rules* and the *Apocalypse Commentary*. An awareness of the remarkable concentration upon apocalyptic-type texts in the *Book of Rules* opens up new questions about the relationship between the *Book of Rules* and the lost *Apocalypse Commentary*.

Lines of investigation that were more historically oriented were initiated by Paul Monceaux and by W.H.C. Frend. Monceaux concentrated on the literary heritage of the African Church, and devoted a considerable section of the fifth volume of his series to a survey of the work of Tyconius.[26]

---

[25]Steinhauser, *The Apocalypse Commentary of Tyconius,* 2.

[26]P. Monceaux, *Histoire Litteraire de l'Afrique Chretienne: Depuis les origines jusqu'a l'invasion arabe* (7 vols; Paris: 1901-1923).

Frend focused upon the social and political history, and undertook archaeological surveys in his study of the North African communities. His work on the Donatist Church provides an essential historical framework for Tyconian studies.[27]

Traugott Hahn published his *Tyconius-Studien* in 1900, and in so doing channelled the interest in the Donatist writer toward ecclesiology.[28] More than half of his study was devoted to Tyconius' notion of the Church. This interest has not flagged in the intervening period. The mid-fifties saw important studies in this area by Joseph Ratzinger[29] and Karl Forster.[30] Where Hahn had stressed the similar elements in the ecclesiology of Augustine and Tyconius, Ratzinger emphasized the differences between the two African thinkers.[31] These differences particularly concerned Augustine's notion of the invisible and the visible Church,[32] and his refusal of Tyconius' key ecclesiological concept, the "bipartite" nature of the Church.[33] For

---

[27]W.H.C. Frend, *The Donatist Church* (Oxford: Clarendon Press, 1952). *The Rise of Christianity* (Philadelphia: Fortress Press, 1984).

[28]T. Hahn, *Tyconius-Studien.* vol. VI, no. 2. (Studien zur Geschichte der Theologie und der Kirche Leipzig: Dietrich, 1900). In Hahn's 116 page study of Tyconius's thought, over half the material was devoted to the study of Tyconius' ecclesiology: "Die Kirche" 57-116.

[29]Joseph Ratzinger, "Beobachtungen zum Kirchenbegriff des Tyconius im 'Liber regularum.'" *Revue des Études Augustinniennes* 2 (1956) 173-186.

[30]Karl Forster, "Die ekkesiologische Bedeutung des Corpus-Begriffes im Liber Regularum des Tyconius." *Muenchener Theologische Zeitschrift* 7 (1956) 173-183.

[31]Ratzinger, "Beobachtungen zum Kirchenbegriff," 173-4.

[32]Ratzinger, "Beobachtungen zum Kirchenbegriff," 175.

[33]Ratzinger, "Beobachtungen zum Kirchenbegriff," 183.

Tyconius, the Church was a mysterious duality of good and evil in one body; for Augustine, the evil ones only *seem* to belong to the Church. Forster suggested that Tyconius' bipartite concept of the Church can be understood from the point of view of the difference between an "ontological" member- ship of the Church and an "ethical" membership.[34]   It is noteworthy that throughout these studies Tyconian ecclesiology was investigated primarily in Augustinian categories.

The dominance of Augustinian interests in Tyconian studies is a fact of contemporary scholarship. There are two main areas of interest: first, what can be learned about Tyconius from the references to the Donatist the- ologian in Augustine's writings,[35] and second, in what way Tyconius may have influenced the thought of Augustine. These questions are well repre- sented in Augustinian scholarship, in the studies of Pincherle[36] and Monceaux,[37] as well as in the biographical studies of Augustine by Peter Brown[38] and G. Bonner.[39] Again within the ambiance of Augustinian stud-

---

[34]Forster, "Die ekkesiologische Bedeutung," 175.

[35]Among the numerous references and quotations: *Ep.* 41; 42; 43; 93; 249., *De Doctrina Christiana* III 30-37; *Retract.* 2:18; *Quaest. in Hept.* 2: 47, 102.

[36]A. Pincherle, "Da Ticonio a Sant' Agostine." *Ricerche Reliogiose.* I (1925) 443-446.

[37]P. Monceaux, *Histoire Littéraire de L'Afrique Chrétienne* V, (Paris: Leroux, 1920) 210-219.

[38]P. Brown, *St. Augustine of Hippo: A Biography* (Berkeley: University of California Press, 1967).

[39]G. Bonner, *St. Augustine of Hippo* (London: SCM Press, 1963). See also H. A. van Bavel, "Tyconius, Augustinus ante Augustinum." *Nieuw Theologisch Tijdschrift* 19 (1930) 36-57.

ies, Brown and W. Babcock have pointed to the significant contribution of Tyconius to the Pauline commentaries, especially the Epistle to the Romans.[40] Peter Brown points to the importance of the Pauline influence on both Augustine and Tyconius.

> The last decades of the fourth century in the Latin church, could well be called "the generation of S. Paul": a common interest in S. Paul drew together widely differing thinkers, and made them closer to each other than to their predecessors. In Italy, Paul had already received commentaries from the Christian Platonist, Marius Victorinus, and from an anonymous layman, probably a retired bureaucrat, known to us as "Ambrosiaster". In Africa, an interest in Paul had brought the Donatist layman, Tyconius, closer to Augustine than to his own bishops.[41]

A review of the principal studies of Tyconius during the past century reveals that Burkitt's hope for a "recognition of the very important place which Tyconius holds in the history of biblical interpretation" has not been fulfilled. There are indications that this omission is being redressed. Where Barnabas Reardon concentrated upon the third rule "of the Promises and the Law" in a dissertation in 1968,[42] more recently Douglas Anderson completed

---

[40]W. Babcock, "Augustine and Tyconius: A Study in the Latin Appropriation of Paul," *Studia Patristica* 17 Part III, (1982) 1209-1215. See also P. Brown, *Augustine of Hippo : A Biography* (Berkley: University of California Press, 1967) 151.

[41]Brown, 151.

[42]B. Reardon, *The Function of Tyconius' Third Hermeneutical Rule* (unpublished Licentiate thesis, Pontifical Biblical Institute, Rome 1968).

an introduction and translation of *The Book of Rules*, the first in a modern language.[43] Karl Froehlich included a translation of the first three rules in his source book of early Christian exegetical works.[44]

The present work is representative of this renewed interest in the *Book of Rules* as an object of scholarly research in its own right. It has been argued that the *Book of Rules* has been an "unread" classic, that is, it was either read through summaries or it was used as a scholarly tool for a variety of purposes other than the one its author intended. Burkitt argued correctly that the *Book of Rules* had been unread for centuries because of the poor textual transmission, but since the fine edition was published a hundred years ago, this obstruction to the reading of Tyconius has been removed.

In the past century, it has continued to be neglected because for all its originality, perceptiveness, and its persuasive logic, the book has been approached in a piecemeal fashion with scholars bearing away what interested them, or continuing to read through the eyes of Augustine. Essentially it has been neglected in the present century because there has been insufficient attention to Tyconius' stated purpose and to the careful development of the argument from point to point, and from chapter to chapter. Attention to the purpose and the inner logic of the *Book of Rules* will be the goal of the present research.

What is it like to read the *Book of Rules* in its "unabridged" form? At first encounter, apart from the elegantly wrought prologue, the impression

---

[43]D.L. Anderson, *The Book of Rules of Tyconius: An Introduction and Translation with Commentary* (Dissertation, Southern Baptist Theological Seminary, Louisville, 1974; Ann Arbor: University Microfilms, 1974).

[44]K. Froehlich, *Biblical Interpretation in the Early Church.*

is that of a rather prosaic text, terse and logical, interspersed with countless scriptural citations of varying lengths. Didactic in style and intent, the *Book of Rules* directs the attention of the reader to the problems posed by certain "obscurities" one encounters in the biblical text. While some commentators have complained that the argument seems digressive at times, and the terminology idiosyncratic, yet even upon a first reading the overall impression of the work agrees with the author's stated purpose of drawing up a guide for the interpretation of the Scriptures.

> ut quis prophetiae inmensam silvam perambulans his regulis quodam modo lucis tramitibus deductus ab errore defendatur
>
> . . . so that on the way through the immense forest of prophecy, guided as it were by paths of light, one would be protected against error (LR 1: 9).

However, in pursuing the logic of the exposition, one becomes aware of deeper currents within the very structure of the argument. It is noticeable that the most problematic and "obscure" passages upon which the author lavishes attention are those which bear upon the mystery of good and evil within the Church. While at one level, the *Book of Rules* remains what it purports to be, a guide for scriptural interpretation, at another level, his theory of scriptural interpretation is integrally related to his theology of the Church.

A further dimension that becomes apparent in both the structure and content of the *Book of Rules* is that, for all its sober tone and clear didactic style, there is a pastoral urgency that permeates the whole work. It may seem paradoxical that the earliest handbook of hermeneutics in the Latin Church appears at the same time under the guise of a pastoral exhortation, addressed both to the Church at large and to the individual member, to search the Scriptures, to pray for the gift of understanding, and to respond to the prophetic admonition to beware of the constant presence of evil that might separate any member from Christ.

The plan of the present study is first to ask what Tyconius meant by "the forest of prophecy" through which one needed guidance, then to explore the "logic" of the "mystical" rules which Tyconius announces in the preamble. Next is the question concerning the structure of the *Book of Rules* itself. Is there a "logic" in the ordering of the chapters? Finally, there will be an attempt to analyze the principles and the sources of the hermeneutical theory proposed by Tyconius. In short the present research is an exploration, on its own terms, of a multilevelled work which Augustine himself characterized as *tam elaborato atque utili operi,* "so elaborate and useful."[45]

---

[45] Augustine, *De Doctrina Christiana,* III, 30.

CHAPTER TWO

THE IMMENSE FOREST OF PROPHECY

THE PREAMBLE TO THE BOOK OF RULES

> No part of a book is so intimate as the Preface. Here, after the long labor of the work is over, the author descends from his platform, and speaks with his reader as man to man, disclosing his hopes and fears, seeking sympathy for his difficulties, offering defence or defiance, according to his temper, against the criticisms which he anticipates. It thus happens that a personality which has been veiled by a formal method throughout many chapters is suddenly seen face to face in the Preface.[1]

Little is known of Tyconius. From Gennadius' account in *De Viris Inlustribus*, we learn that Tyconius was an African, a Donatist, well-educated, an ecclesiastical writer, and a scriptural commentator. From Augustine we learn of Tyconius' conflicts with the Donatist bishop of Carthage, Parmenian, in the late seventies. After the death of Parmenian in 391, the Catholic party continued to discuss the thought of Tyconius, but it was to the books rather than to the man that they refer.

What does his single surviving book, the *Book of Rules,* reveal of Tyconius' personality? While there has been disagreement about the compositional features of the work, particularly with regard to Tyconius' intention in the order of the seven rules, there is a general consensus about the forceful, logical style of the writing. It is a sparse style, minimalistic at

---

[1]C.W. Eliot, ed., *Prefaces and Prologues to Famous Books* (The Harvard Classics, Danbury, Connecticut: Grolier, 1890, 1938, 1910).

times, with every word weighted for value. It is a style calculated to persuade by reasonableness rather than to charm by elegant touches.

The foregoing observations on the sober style of the *Book of Rules* have to be balanced by an appreciative glance at Tyconius' preamble. The delicate juxtaposition of the syntactical forms, the contrasting images of light and darkness, of openings and closings, are woven into an intricate unity to express, with the utmost economy, the author's conviction of the importance of understanding the "logic" of the "mystical rules" which *obtinent* "withhold" *aliquibus* "from some" *universae legis recessus* "the hidden parts of the universal law" (LR 1: 5).

Chapter Five of the present study will examine the preamble more closely; for the moment it is enough to suggest that the most obvious starting place for an introduction to the *Book of Rules* is Tyconius' own introduction. This finely wrought preamble was prefixed to Augustine's own summary of the *Book of Rules* in the third book of the *De Doctrina Christiana*. Augustine's criticism of Tyconius' pretensions (as Augustine understood them) to solve all the obscurities of Scripture by a mere *seven* rules has been virtually the only attempt to evaluate Tyconius' purpose in writing the *Book of Rules*.

TYCONIUS' PREAMBLE

> Necessarium duxi ante omnia quae mihi videntur libellum regularem
> scribere, et secretorum legis veluti claves et luminaria fabricare.
> Sunt enim quaedam regulae mysticae quae universae legis recessus
> obtinent et veritatis thesauros aliquibus invisibiles faciunt; quarum
> si ratio regularum sine invidia ut communicamus accepta fuerit,
> clausa quaeque patefient et obscura dilucidabuntur, ut quis prophetiae

inmensam silvam perambulans his regulis quodam modo lucis tramitibus deductus ab errore defendatur. (LR 1:1-9)

All things considered I found it necessary to write an essay about the rules, and to fabricate, so to speak, keys and windows appropriate to the secrets of the Law. There are certain mystical rules which withhold the hidden parts of the universal Law and render invisible for some people the treasures of the truth; should the logic of these rules be recognized as readily as we communicate it, then anything closed would be opened, and what is dark would be illuminated, so that walking through the immense forest of prophecy, guided as it were on paths of light, one would be protected against error.

Before tackling the thorny question of what Tyconius meant by "certain mystical rules"[2] which render the "treasures of truth" invisible to some people, it is important to note what the author hopes will be the result of his labors: if the "logic of these rules" be recognized, then one would not be lost in the "immense forest of prophecy." What does Tyconius mean by the "forest of prophecy"? Is this a general term for the Scriptures, since he spoke of the "mystical rules" withholding "the hidden parts of the universal Law"? Does he mean the Old Testament, or perhaps more specifically, the books of the Prophets?

Burkitt argues that "the immense forest of prophecy" is to be identified with what he terms "the enormous residuum" of prophetic texts that had never been interpreted by the early Church.

In this work Tyconius attempts to deal with a real problem. The Church had inherited the Old Testament and held fast to the belief

---

[2]See Chapter Five.

that the ancient scriptures wholly testified to the New Covenant. Many Jewish prophecies are appealed to by the New Testament writers, by the early apologists, and in such works as S. Cyprian's *Testimonia*. But there still remained an enormous residuum which was not obviously edifying, so that many verses from the Prophets have been quoted by no ancient writer. It was this unsurveyed region, the "prophetiae inmensa silua," which Tyconius set himself to explore and map out. Consequently his longer quotations are often from passages which no one else has touched. His aim was to find general rules of interpretation which would cover every case, and which therefore might be applied to the most unpromising subjects and images. Whatever we may think of his results, they certainly seemed to meet the wants of the men of his own time.[3]

What of Burkitt's contention that in the *Book of Rules* Tyconius was providing a systematic frame for the exegesis of the many prophetic texts so often neglected by Christian exegetes because of the problem of understanding their relevance for the community? It would be instructive to explore the prior history of the exegesis of the texts that Tyconius cites in the *Book of Rules*, but the more immediate task is to study what texts Tyconius selected for comment and why they were selected. Rather than be guided by Burkitt's speculation about Tyconius' purpose, it seems more appropriate to start examining what Tyconius meant by the "immense forest of prophecy" with the data that Burkitt himself provides in his index of Tyconius' biblical citations.

---

[3]Burkitt, *Book of Rules*, xiii.

The following tabulation simply notes the books of the bible that are represented in the *Book of Rules* and the number of verses cited from each book by Tyconius. In broadest terms we are asking if there is a general spread of citations throughout the Scriptures, or whether there is a concentration of attention in any particular area.

OLD TESTAMENT QUOTATIONS

Book	no. of verses cited

(a) *The Pentateuch*

Genesis	28
Exodus	9
Leviticus	1
Numbers	1
Deuteronomy	0
Total = 39	

Comment: Genesis is the most frequently quoted book of the Pentateuch, with 17 of its 28 verses concerning the sons of Abraham.

Book	no. of verses cited

(b) *The Historical Books*

Joshua	2
2 Kings	7
3 Kings	11
1 Chronicles	1
Total=21	

Comment: The historical books are quoted infrequently with the exception of references to God's promise of the kingdom to David's sons (2 Kings and 3 Kings).

Book   no. of verses cited

(c) *The Wisdom Books*
    Job   3
    Psalms   34
    Proverbs   2
    Ecclesiastes   2
    Canticle   5
    Wisdom of Solomon   10
    Sirach   1
              Total=57

Comment: The frequency of the quotations from the psalms is hardly surprising, but the importance of the Wisdom of Solomon and the Canticle is noteworthy.

Book   no. of verses cited

(d) *The Prophets*
    The major prophets
    Isaiah   124
    Jeremiah   36
    Lamentations   1
    Ezekiel   143
    Daniel   7
              Total=311
    The minor prophets
    Hosea   3
    Amos   4
    Micah   1
    Joel   2
    Obediah   2
    Jonah   1
    Nahum   3
    Zephaniah   8
    Haggai   3
    Zechariah   9
    Malachi   1
              Total=37

Comment: In round numbers we note that of the 450 Old Testament verses, 350 were from the books of the Prophets. While there is an obvious concentration on the prophetic literature, at the same time even here there is a selective focus. In sheer number of citations Ezekiel is the favored prophetic text, even over Isaiah. A closer look at the Ezekiel texts demonstrates an even finer focus on chapters 20-39 which speak of the judgments against the nations. Chapters 40-48 which refer to the glory of the rebuilt Temple are ignored in the *Book of Rules*. The seven quotations from the book of Daniel echo these themes, the coming judgment, the "abomination of desolation" in the Temple, and the last king exalting himself above every god (Dan 7:10; 11:31, 36, 38).

The calculation of the actual numbers of verses cited in the *Book of Rules* gives some indication of the attention to the books of the Prophets, but this "raw score" does not take into account the sheer bulk of material devoted to the exegesis of these prophetic texts. Burkitt's critical edition of the *Book of Rules* runs to 85 pages. Of these, 16 pages are occupied by Rule VII, and Rule VII is basically a line-by-line commentary on two prophetic texts – Isaiah 14: 12-21 and Ezekiel 28:1-19.

NEW TESTAMENT QUOTATIONS

Book	no. of verses cited
The Gospels	
Matthew	40
Mark	2
Luke	11
John	20
	Total = 73

Comment: The Gospel of Matthew is the favored text, and within this gospel the eschatological sections of the gospel receive most attention, namely eschatological "signs" in Matt 24.

Book	no. of verses cited
Acts, Epistles, Apocalypse	
Acts	2
Romans	61
1 Corinthians	17
2 Corinthians	17
Galatians	26
Ephesians	12
Philippians	4
Colossians	5
1 Thessalonians	1
2 Thessalonians	8
1 Timothy	2
2 Timothy	3
Titus	1
1 Peter	1
1 John	15
The Apocalypse	15
	Total=190

Comment: In round numbers, of the 260 New Testament verses, over 150 are from the Pauline epistles. Romans and Galatians dominate the selection, but the mere counting of verses does not do justice to the significance of 2 Thessalonians. Here the focus is on the second chapter concerning the revelation of the Antichrist (2 Thess 2:3, five times; 2 Thess 2:7, four times).

The quotations from the Apocalypse have special significance if only because of the importance of Tyconius' *Commentary on the Apocalypse*. In the *Book of Rules* Tyconius draws from chapters 1 and 2 of the Apocalypse, the seven letters to the Churches and from chapters 9-12, the opening of the seventh seal and the prophecies with regard to the Antichrist. As in the book of Ezekiel, where Tyconius omitted any reference to the reconstruction of the Temple, here in the Apocalypse, he makes no reference to the New Jerusalem. The focus is upon the coming and the destruction of the Antichrist.

TEXTS IN CONTEXT IN THE BOOK OF RULES

The preceding analysis allows us to look again at the question of what Tyconius meant by the "immense forest of prophecy." The scriptural citations in the *Book of Rules* are taken both from the Old and the New Testament. Although there is a striking concentration upon the books of the Prophets, the degree of attention given to the New Testament books, especially the Pauline letters, makes it difficult to accept Burkitt's identification of the "forest of prophecy" with the books of the Prophets, themselves.

The foregoing analysis, though helpful, is just a preliminary step in the analysis of Burkitt's index of the scriptural quotations of the *Book of Rules*. It would be a task beyond the scope of the present work to analyze each quotation in its context, but Tyconius' clear, logical style enables us to follow the argument in each chapter of the *Book of Rules* and to note the biblical texts he chooses to illustrate the step-by-step development of his theory of scriptural exegesis.

Rule I – Of the Lord and His Body

In Rule I, texts are selected according to the christological, ecclesiological or eschatological focus of the argument.

Passages long familiar to Tyconius' readers for their christological interpretation are chosen from the Isaian "servant songs" (Isa 53:4, 5, 6, LR 2:4), from the Book of Daniel (Dan 2:34, 35 LR 2:15), and from the Psalms (Ps 110, LR 7:10).

Texts that are central to the ecclesiastical argument of Rule I – the mystery of the union of Christ and His Body, the Church – are drawn from the New Testament epistles (Eph 2:21, LR 7:25; Eph 4:15, 16, LR 3:4; Eph 5:31, 32, LR 7:13).

A focus upon the title, Son of Man, establishes the eschatological frame for a further group of texts concerning both the coming of the Son of Man (Matt 26:64, LR 4:16; 1 Thess 2:19 LR 6:8) and the coming of the Antichrist "in the midst" of the Church (1 John 2:18, LR 5:1; 2 Thess 2:3, 4, 7, LR 5:15,16; 8:2).

The selective movement from general christological and ecclesiological concerns to the particular emphasis on an eschatology, and then on to a series of texts referring to the revelation of the "man of sin" (2 Thess 2:7) who is "coming" "in the midst" of the Church establishes a pattern that may be observed throughout the *Book of Rules*.

Rule II – Of the Bipartite Body

Rule II introduces the central concept of Tyconius' ecclesiology, the "bipartite" nature of the Church; that is, the Church is composed of good and evil membership. The majority of the biblical citations in Rule II come from the Book of Isaiah. A series of prophecies directed at Israel alternates between promise and warning (Isa 33:20, LR 10:7; Isa 33:23, LR 10:10; Isa 42:16, 17, LR 9:1; Isa 43:5-8, LR 9:7; Isa 43:27-44: 1, LR 9:6).

This duality of promise and threat directed at the same referent also governs the selection of texts from Matthew (Matt 24:26 ff., LR 11:6) and from Romans (Rom 2:24, LR 10:17).

According to Tyconius, this pattern of praise and blame addressed to the same referent reveals the good and evil membership in the one Body, the Church.

Rule III – Of Promise and the Law

Rule III is a magisterial commentary on the Pauline themes of promise and law, of faith and works, of free will and predestination, which captured the attention of later commentators beginning with Augustine; but

Tyconius' attention does not waver from *his* constant theme of the "doubleness" of the Church, especially the presence of its evil membership. As would be expected in this Rule, the heaviest concentration of texts is from Romans and Galatians, especially Romans, chapters 3, 4, 7, and 8 and Galatians, chapters 2, 3, and 4.

A series of texts from the Genesis accounts of the promises to Abraham, and of the opposition between Ishmael and Isaac, and between Jacob and Esau are related to the themes in Romans and that of Galatians (Gen 15:1, LR 23:23; Gen 22:18, 16, LR 23:2; 28:28).

From Isaiah, texts are selected referring to the "giftedness" of salvation rather than any thought of personal merit (Isa 1:19 LR 24:7; Isa 48:18, 19, LR 26:19; 28:7).

From the Gospel of Matthew comes a series of texts which emphasizes the "separateness" of good and evil (Matt 6:10, 3 LR 17:14; Matt 13:30, LR 19:12). This theme of "separateness" is defined more sharply in the first Epistle of John (1 John 4:3, LR 30:26; 1 John 4:18, LR 25:14), and finally it is presented in its starkest contrasts in the second Epistle to the Thessalonians in the discernment of the presence of the Antichrist "in the midst" of the Church (2 Thess 2:3, LR 30:27; 31:4; 2 Thess 2:7, LR 30:27; 2 Thess 2:8, LR 3:11; 2 Thess 2:9, LR 30:28).

Rule IV – Of Species and Genus

Rule IV is concerned with the ecclesiological interpretation of prophecies ("genus" prophecies) addressed to individuals, to cities, or to nations ("species" prophecies).

While there are references to the city of Cain (Gen 4:17, LR 42:9) and to the promises made to the kings of Israel (2 Kgs 7:12-16 LR 37:12; 2 Kgs 7:14, 15 LR 38:27), the main texts are drawn from Isaiah, Ezekiel and

Jeremiah concerning oracles against Babylon, against Tyre, Egypt, and also oracles describing the purging of evil from Jerusalem. Isaiah chapters 13 and 14 are directed to Babylon; chapter 19 to Egypt; and chapter 23 to Tyre. Ezekiel, chapter 20, speaks to Jerusalem; chapter 27 to Tyre; while the Jeremiah texts refer to the beginning of the purge of Jerusalem (Jer 25:15-29, LR 53, 54).

Very few texts in Rule IV come from the Gospels, but Tyconius again draws from the second Epistle to the Thessalonians (2 Thess 2:3, LR 50:10; 2 Thess 2:7, LR 52:9), and from the Apocalypse (Rev 11:8, LR 50:8). A final citation from Ephesians reinforces the familiar themes of evil within the Church (Eph 6:12, LR 54:23). The fight of the saints is against "spiritual wickedness in heavenly places." Tyconius calls the Church the "spiritual world" (LR 61:31).

Rule V – Of Times

Rule V concerns the computation of time in the Scripture. Attention is devoted to the meaning of "day" in the early chapters of Genesis (Gen 1:5, 14, 16, LR 56:25; 58:27; 57:9) as well as in the duration of the deluge (Gen 7:4, LR 64:30; Gen 8:4, 5, LR 65:17). From Exodus, Tyconius selects texts that refer to the time Israel spent in Egypt (Exod 1:6-10, LR 55:13; Exod 12:40, LR 55:9). Texts from the Gospels discuss the computation of the "three days" between the crucifixion and the resurrection (Matt 28:1, LR 57:14).

The long quotation from Jeremiah 17:19-27 (LR 62:7) on the question of the special quality of Sabbath time reintroduces the Tyconian theme of evil within the Church. Luke 4:19 (LR 60:16, 21; 65:20) and 2 Corinthians 6:2 (LR 60:15,19) tell us that *now* is the "acceptable time" for the repentance of sinners.

The eschatological concerns so evident in the preceding chapters of the *Book of Rules* are represented in Rule V by texts selected from Matthew (Matt 11:28, LR 63:36; Matt 12:40, LR 56:20, 57:30, 59:8; Matt 19:28, LR 60:7; Matt 26:64, LR 43:5) and from 1 John (1 John 2:18, LR 60:15).

Rule V devotes special attention to the Apocalypse. Just as the souls "under the altar" ask "how long?" at the opening of the fifth seal (Rev 6:9,10), in Rule V, Tyconius focuses on the duration of the "tribulation" (Rev 1:4, LR 59:24; Rev 2:10, LR 60:9; Rev 9:10, LR 60:25; Rev 11:2, LR 61:3; Rev 11:3, LR 60:28; Rev 11:8, 9, LR 61:8; Rev 12:14, LR 61:5).

Rule VI – Of Recapitulation

Rule VI concerns the discernment of the signs of the coming judgment and the separation of the good from the bad. Except for a scattering of texts from the psalms (Ps 64:12, LR 60:22; Ps 67:18, LR 60:4; Ps 104:8, LR 60:5; Ps 105:1-3, LR 67:16), the citations are from the New Testament. This underlines the fact that the "immense forest of prophecy" is not to be identified with the Old Testament as a whole or with the books of the prophets in particular.

Except for the citation of Luke 17:29-32 (referring to the destruction of Sodom), the Gospel quotations are taken from Matthew. Matthew 24:15, 16 (LR 67:8) directs attention to the "sign" of the prophet Daniel, the "abomination of desolation" in the Temple. Tyconius claims that there is a "likeness" of this sign already happening "in Africa" (LR 67:11). Other texts from Matthew speak of the separation between good and bad that is already a reality in the Church. "Not everyone who says to me, 'Lord, Lord,' will enter the Kingdom of Heaven" (Matt 7:21, LR 69:4). Those who persecute their brethren in the Church persecute their Lord (Matt 25:40, LR 68:21).

The remaining citations are from the epistles, notably the first Epistle of John which speaks of the signs for discerning who is "separate from Jesus" through hatred of their fellow Christian (1 John 3:14, 15, LR 68:26; 1 John 4:1-3, LR 67:31). Once again 2 Thessalonians 2:3 is cited -- the "separation" and the "revelation" of the "man of sin" (LR 67:14).

Rule VII – Of the Devil and His Body

Rule VII concentrates on the exegesis of two long texts, the first from Isaiah (Isa 14:12-21, LR 70:11-77:14), describing the blasphemies and the destruction of the King of Babylon who thought to place his throne in the heavens. The second is from Ezekiel (Ezek 28:1-17, LR 77:15-85:27), the lament for the Prince of Tyre, adorned with jewels and claiming to be as God in the "heart of the sea." The rest of the biblical texts cited in Rule VII reflect these themes of judgment.

From Genesis, Tyconius selects Genesis 3:22, 24 (LR 81:20) where the "flaming sword" separates the evil-doers from the tree of life. Also from Genesis, Tyconius quotes the destruction of Sodom and Gomorrah (Gen 19:23, 24, LR 85:2) and the salvation of Lot "from the midst" of the evil cities (LR 85:7).

In the Gospel of Matthew, Tyconius concentrates on the parables that speak of the coming judgment (Matt 6:20, 21, LR 82:33; Matt 12:35, LR 84:24; Matt 13:28, 39, LR 79:2, 79:3; Matt 22:11ff., LR 83:26). The revelation of the Antichrist is cited from 2 Thessalonians (2 Thess 2:6-8, LR 74:26; 2 Thess 2:7, LR 84:32).

Since in the major Isaian text (Isa 14:12ff.) the King of Babylon had been compared to "Lucifer" the morning star, Tyconius cites the verses from the Apocalypse which refer to Christ, the true "morning star" (Rev 2:26, LR 71:28; Rev 22:16,17, LR 71:26). Revelation 17:4 (LR 82:25), in describing the harlot Babylon, adorned with jewels, brings together images and references from both the Isaian and Ezekiel texts around which the whole chapter has been shaped.

The preceding survey of texts in context in the *Book of Rules*, while sketched in broad outline, is sufficiently delineated to argue that the scriptural citations in the *Book of Rules* are not so much selected from a particular area of Scripture – the Old Testament, the New Testament, the books of the Prophets. Rather they are focused upon the Scriptures that evoke eschatological themes of the coming separation of the good and the evil. Even more, there is a focus upon texts that refer to the presence of evil-doers among the nations, or in Jerusalem itself, evil-doers outside of the Church or those "separate from Jesus" even among the "brethren."

ANTICHRIST - IN THE MIDST OF THE CHURCH

In Rule I, Tyconius introduces texts that refer to the coming of the Son of Man (Matt 26:64, 24:30) and then follows with a series of texts that refer to the coming of the Antichrist (1 John 2:18; 2 Cor 11:4; Matt 24:4; 2 Thess 2:4; Dan 11:36, 11:31; Matt 24:15; 2 Cor 11:2; 2 Thess 2:3). The chapter concludes with a warning to remain watchful for the coming of the Antichrist – that "abomination of desolation" already to be found "in the midst" of the temple which is destined to be destroyed (2 Thess 2:3, 4; Matt 24:15; Dan 9:31). There must be a constant awareness of evil "in the midst" until the Church departs "from the midst."

These two phrases, "in the midst" and "from the midst" become the linchpin for Tyconius' ecclesiology. He argues that the Church is "bipartite," that is, composed of both good and evil membership, and that this evil is a secret presence "in the midst" only to be fully revealed at the coming of Christ in glory. The usurped temple in which the Antichrist has set his throne (Matt 24:15; Dan 9:31) will be destroyed, and the separation of the good and evil will be effected when those who are united to Christ are taken "from the midst" of the threatened destruction.

This biblical image of the Antichrist enthroned "in the midst," in 2 Thessalonians 2:7, attracts a whole network of texts from the Old Testament, not only the reference about the "abomination of desolation" in Daniel (Dan 9:31) but also texts from Isaiah and Ezekiel. In Rule IV (LR 47:27), the citation of Isaiah 24:1-13 breaks off at the point where the prophet refers to the desolation "in the midst of the people" *in medio gentium* (Isa 24:13). The whole of Rule VII is dominated by the exegesis of the two oracles of judgment against the King of Babylon and the Prince of Tyre. In Isaiah 14:12-21, the King of Babylon has set his throne in the heavens. In Ezekiel 28:1-19, the Prince of Tyre occupies a throne in the "heart of the sea" and in the "midst of the stones of fire" *in medio lapidum igneorum.*

THE DEPARTURE OF THE CHURCH – FROM THE MIDST"

This image of evil established "in the midst" of the Church is counterbalanced by a second biblical image, the departure of the saved "from the midst." As Lot, the one just man, departs "from the midst" *(et emisit Lot e medio subversionis)* of the destruction of Sodom (Gen 19:15-17, LR 85:12), so too will the faithful members of the Church depart "from the midst" of the destruction of the doomed temple where the Antichrist has enthroned himself (LR 8:2).

Tyconius cites 2 Thessalonians 2:7, "He who *now* takes hold (of Christ), *then* (at the judgment) he will come 'from the midst.'" Again, in Rule VII (LR 84:31) in the citation of Ezekiel 28:18, Tyconius argues that the "fiery stones" that are the true sons and daughters of the Church will be taken "from the midst," while the precious stones stolen from Christ by Satan will be left "in the midst" of the general destruction.

In his study of the reception and the history of the *Apocalypse Commentary* of Tyconius, Steinhauser notes that Jerome had revised the millenarian interpretations of the earlier commentary on the Apocalypse of Victorinus of Pettau with Tyconius' *Commentary*. In this revised Victorine commentary, there is a reference to the departure of the Church "from the midst" of the destruction, in a commentary on Revelation 15:1 referring to the last seven plagues "when the church will go out from the midst" *cum ecclesia de medio exierit.*

To return to the question posed at the beginning of the chapter, what does Tyconius intend by "the immense forest of prophecy" through which the reader will be guided along "paths of light?" We have yet to examine what Tyconius means by these "paths of light," but from the preceding analysis of the texts commented upon by Tyconius it may be argued that the "prophecies" of the *Book of Rules* are those passages throughout the Scriptures that concern the mystery of evil, always active, always "separate from Jesus." It is a secret presence, and one that Tyconius insists can only be revealed by the grace of God (LR 4:11).

The purpose of the *Book of Rules* is to provide a systematic frame for the interpretation of these prophecies. It is very easy to go astray in such an "immense forest." One needs to be aware of the "logic" of the seven "mystical" rules found throughout Scripture, so that the interpreter of these difficult texts will not be among those for whom the "mystical" rules render the "treasures of truth" invisible.

CHAPTER THREE

THE LOGIC OF THE MYSTICAL RULES

In the preamble (LR 1:1-9) to the *Book of Rules*, Tyconius claims that in writing a book of rules *libellum regularem scribere*, he is in effect making "keys or windows for the secrets of the Law" *secretorum legis veluti claves et luminaria fabricare*. Tyconius lays special stress on the secrets of Scripture, what is "shut" *clausa*, what is "obscured" *obscura*. Tyconius encourages his readers by promising them that "if the logic of these rules is accepted," then what is shut will be opened and what is obscured will be illumined. The immediate practical purpose of the *Book of Rules* is to explain the "logic" *ratio regularum* of the seven "mystical rules" *regulae mysticae* which hold these secrets.

Before examining Tyconius' explanation of the "logic" of the individual rules, we take a brief look at the understanding of the task of hermeneutics in the ancient Church in relation to what were regarded as the "obscurities" of Scripture.

THE OBSCURITIES OF SCRIPTURE

Christian interpreters of the early centuries of the Church were heirs to already long and complex classical and Jewish hermeneutical traditions. The sacred writings of the ancient world were the repositories of wisdom and guidance. Especially as *written*, the ancient poetry and oracles acquired a particular fixed, sacral character, and the study of the texts themselves gave rise to highly sophisticated methods of interpretation in religio-philosophical circles.

> I consider that the chief part of a man's education is to be skilled in
> epic poetry; and this means that he should be able to understand
> what the poets have said, and whether they have said it rightly or
> not, and to know how to draw distinctions, and to give an answer
> when a question is put to him.[1]

Under schools of commentators on the ancient texts, the piety and the knowledge of the inspired authors were defended. Among the textual critics, hermeneutics developed a double task: first to explain the enigmatic or even offensive elements in the old mythic material – the "obscurities" – and second, in that very process to grasp the "inner meaning" of the text. Hermeneutics was a task, a labour, but a labour of love as the interpreter moved through the intricacies of the texts discovering in them the treasures of wisdom and insight in the sacred writings.

One of the striking contrasts between hermeneutical works of the ancient and the modern Church lies in the very focus of the attention of the exegete. The presupposition of the interpreter of the ancient Church was that one of the first tasks of hermeneutics was to explore and resolve these "obscurities" of the biblical text. Clement of Alexandria distinguishes between the Christian "Gnostics" and the heretics, who may take "their stand in the name of the Father and the Son, but have no power to bring out the exact perspicuity of the oracles by subtle distinctions and by smoothing away of

---

[1]Plato *Protagoras* 72, 339a (New York: Harper and Brothers Publ., 1957) 52. E. Hatch, *The Influence of Greek Ideas on Christianity.*

difficulties."[2] "Obscurities" occurred when the meaning of the text was uncertain, or, more seriously, when the text, at face value, presented an affront to God or the divine purpose, and so challenged the faith tradition of the community.

This understanding of the task of the Christian interpreter is illustrated by Augustine in the Preface of his *De Doctrina Christiana*, written a little over a decade after the *Book of Rules*.

> There are certain rules for the interpretation of Scripture which I think might, with great advantage, be taught to earnest students of the Word, that they might profit not only from reading the works of others who have laid open the secrets of the sacred writings, but also from themselves opening such secrets to others.[3]

Later in the Preface, Augustine further defends the usefulness of expounding the rules for the interpretation of Scripture.

> Just as he who knows how to read is not dependent on someone else when he finds a book, to tell him what is written in it, so the man who is in possession of the rules which I here attempt to lay down, if he meets with an obscure passage in the books which he reads, will not need an interpreter to lay open the secret to him, but holding fast by certain rules, and following certain indications, will ar-

---

[2]*Miscellanies* Book VII, F. Hort and J. Major (London: Macmillan and Co., 1902) 192, 193.

[3]Augustine, *On Christian Doctrine*, 510.

rive at the hidden sense without any error, or at least without falling into any gross absurdity.[4]

Augustine's confident proposal of the rules to guide Christian exegesis is a far cry from the wary approach of Tertullian, his fellow North African two centuries earlier. Here in the critical years of Gnostic hermeneutics, Tertullian is only too aware of the fascination of scriptural "obscurities" for the Church of his time, and the very real danger posed by Gnostic "spiritual" interpretations to the "historical" realities of the Gospel.

In his fight against the Gnostic "moralizing" interpretation of the resurrection of the dead, Tertullian had insisted upon the importance of the literal meaning of the text and of the historical reality of the events described, whether it be the actual downfall of nations and cities in the Old Testament or the healing miracles of Jesus in the gospel.

> The realities are involved in the words, just as the words are read in the realities. Thus, [we find that] the allegorical style is not used in all parts of the prophetic record, although it occasionally occurs in certain portions of it.[5]

Tertullian uses this occasion to discuss the problem of "obscurities" in Scripture.

> First what must be the meaning of so many important passages of Holy Scriptures, which so obviously attest the resurrection of the

---

[4] Augustine, *On Christian Doctrine*, 521.

[5] Tertullian, *On the Resurrection of the Flesh*, trans. Dr. Holmes, *Latin Christianity: Its Founder, Tertullian*, ed. A. Roberts and J. Donaldson (The Ante-Nicene Fathers; Grand Rapids, MI: Wm Eerdmans, 1963) 559.

bodies, as to admit not even the appearance of a figurative significa-
tion? Indeed since some passages are more obscure than others it
cannot but be right that uncertain statements should be determined
by certain ones, and obscure ones by such as are clear and plain, else
there is fear that, in the conflict of certainties and uncertainties, of
explicitness and obscurity, faith may be shattered, truth endangered,
and the Divine Being himself be branded as inconstant.[6]

The Alexandrian tradition of exegesis had a very different approach to
obscurities in Scripture. It was a question of the theological understanding of
the formation of the written text of Scripture.

Now, everyone who embraces the word, even the dullest of all, is
convinced that there are certain mystical arrangements *oikonomiai*
which the divine writings reveal to us.[7]

It was a pneumatological question. The Spirit as Author of
Scripture intends these obscurities, and the obscurities themselves have an
important function in the hermeneutical process which can only be exercised
in and through the grace of the Spirit.

In the fourth book of the *Peri Archon*, Origen discusses the
"innumerable errors" which have arisen "because so many people have failed
to find the right path which must govern the exploration of the holy
books."[8]

---

[6]Tertullian, *On the Resurrection of the Flesh*, 560.

[7]Origen, *On First Principles:* IV: 2, 2. Froehlich, *Biblical
Interpretation*, (Philadelphia: Fortress Press, 1984) 56.

[8]Origen, *On First Principles* IV 2, 1. Froehlich, *Biblical
Interpretation*, 54.

The reason for the false opinions, the impious attitudes, and the amateurish talk about God . . . seems to be no other than that Scripture is not understood in its spiritual sense but is interpreted according to the mere letter. All those, therefore, who are convinced that the holy books are not the writings of human authors but were composed and have come down to us as a result of the inspiration of the Holy Spirit by the will of the Father of all through Jesus Christ, and who adhere to the rule of the celestial Church of Christ resting on the succession of the apostles, must be taught what I take to be the correct method of interpretation . . .[9]

Directing attention to legal and historical texts, Origen speaks of "impossibilities," of "stumbling blocks" in the text.

But if the usefulness of the legal prescriptions as well as the logical coherence and the smooth flow of the historical narrative were automatically evident everywhere, we would not believe that it is possible to find some other sense in the Scriptures beside the obvious one. For this reason the Word of God has arranged the insertion of certain offensive features, of stumbling blocks and impossibilities amid the law and the historical narrative. He wanted to avoid that, being totally carried away by the plain text and its unspoiled charm, we either would disregard its teaching altogether because we did not

---

[9]Origen, *On First Principles* IV 2, 2. Froehlich, *Biblical Interpretation*, 56.

find any lessons worthy of God, or would refuse to move beyond the letter and not learn anything more divine.[10]

Origen carefully distinguishes the "plain text," "the bodily element of the scripture," from its inner meaning, the spiritual element. The words of Scripture, like the Incarnate Word, have a duality of body and spirit. Even though there were "stumbling blocks" in the biblical narrative to remind the careful reader to "move beyond the letter."

> The intent was that the external cover of spiritual things, namely, the bodily element of the Scriptures, should not be rendered unprofitable for so many peoples; but rather, that it should be capable of improving the multitude according to their capacity.[11]

Augustine's prayer for understanding the Scriptures reflects the attitude of the Christian interpreter to the task of understanding the "secrets of the Law":

> Be liberal in giving of them [the moments flying away] the time for our meditations on the secrets of Thy Law and do not close it against those who knock (cf. Matt 7:7).

> For, Thou didst not will so many pages of dark secrets to be written in vain; nor are those forests without their stags (cf. Ps 28:9), taking refuge

---

[10]Origen, *On First Principles IV* 2, 9. Froehlich, *Biblical Interpretation,* 62.

[11]Origen, *On First Principles IV* 2, 8. Froehlich, *Biblical Interpretation,* 62.

in them, recovering, walking about and feeding, lying down and ruminating. O Lord, perfect me and reveal those pages to me.[12]

TYCONIUS AND OBSCURITIES OF SCRIPTURE

Even a brief perusal of the *Book of Rules* reveals that Tyconius shares the general understanding of his time that the immediate task of Christian hermeneutics is to address the "obscurities" of the biblical text.

Tyconius claims that there are seven areas of special difficulty in interpreting the prophetic texts of the Old and New Testament, and that in each of these areas one has to be guided by the inner mystery, the "logic" of the "rule," of that aspect of Scripture if one is to traverse the "immense forest of prophecy" without going astray.[13]

Tyconius announces seven "mystical rules":[14]

I. of the Lord and His Body

II. of the Lord's Bipartite Body

III. of Promises and the Law

IV. of Species and Genus

V. of Times

VI. of Recapitulation

VII. of the Devil and His Body

---

[12]Augustine, *Confessions* 11.2, trans. V.J. Bourke (New York: Fathers of the Church, Inc., 1953) 329-330.

[13]LR 1:7, 8.

[14]LR 1:3.

The immediate practical purpose of the *Book of Rules* is to address the problems of interpretation, the "obscurities," in seven "mysteries" of the prophetic texts.

Rule I: problems concerning the interpretation of texts that had been traditionally attributed to Christ, e.g. the Isaian servant Songs (LR 2:3-14), or Christological titles, "Son of Man" "Son of God" (LR 4 -7).

Rule II: problems concerning the prophetic texts which both bless and condemn the same referent, e.g. Israel blessed and cursed in its inheritance (LR 11:13).[15]

Rule III: problems concerning the fidelity of God's promises. How were people "justified" before the coming of Christ? What is the relationship between Law and Promise? In what sense are the divine promises conditional?

Rule IV: problems concerning the interpretation of prophecies addressed to individuals, e.g. Solomon, or the prince of Tyre, or to cities, e.g. Babylon, Jerusalem. What is their continuing relevance?

Rule V: problems of interpreting "time-quantities" in Scripture.

Rule VI: the interpretation of the signs of the Second Coming and subsequent separation of the good and evil membership of the Church.

Rule VII: problems of discerning the presence of Antichrist in the Church.

1. Of the Lord and His Body

The first "rule" concerns the mystery of the union of Christ and His Body, the Church (I Cor 12:27; Eph 1:9, 10). Because of this mystery, the

---

[15]LR 11:12-14. Therefore, all the statements throughout Scripture in which God announces that Israel will perish deservedly or that his inheritance will be cursed must be understood in terms of this mystery.

referent in the prophetic text can be directed either to Christ, the Head, or to the Church His Body. After illustrating the obvious logic of this principle in a series of prophetic texts,[16] Tyconius then introduces instances of greater difficulty.

In other cases such reasoning is less successful because the text can be applied correctly to both, either the Lord or His Body. In such instances the proper meaning can be perceived only by an even greater grace from God. Thus we read in the gospel, "From now on you will see the Son of Man sitting at the right hand of the power and coming on the clouds of Heaven."[17]

The problem, or obscurity, for Tyconius is that while Matthew 26:64 says that "from now on" *a modo* the Son of Man will be seen "coming," an earlier section, Matthew 24:30, claimed "all the nations on the earth will mourn" and then "*tunc* they will see the Son of Man coming on the clouds of heaven."

The obstacle to the logical interpretation presented by the contradictory prophetic statements in Matthew actually functions to alert the reader to the principle that because of the union of Head and Body, the Christological title "Son of Man" can be applied to Christ or to the Church without logical contradiction.

Following the "logic" of the "rule," or the mystery, of the union of Christ and Church, the prophetic texts in Matthew concerning the "comings" of the Son of Man reveal two advents.

---

[16]Isa 53:4-6, 10,11; Dan 2:34, 35; Ps 90:11-16 (LXX); Isa 61:10; Rev 22:17.

[17]LR 4:13-17. Froehlich "Tyconius," *Biblical Interpretation*, 107. Matt 24:64.

Indeed two things must happen: first, the advent of the Body, that is, the Church which is continually coming in one and the same invisible glory; then the advent of the Head, that is, the Lord, in manifest glory.[18]

The two advents, first the Church, continually coming to birth in its membership through baptism, and then the manifest glory of the coming of Christ in the Eschaton, resolve for Tyconius the apparent contradictions of the "from now on" *a modo* Matthew 26:64, and the "then" *tunc*, Matthew 24:30. At the same time there is another "coming" or "growth" in the Church. It is the "growing" of the "opposing body," and the prophetic texts warn us to be on our guard for signs of its insidious growth.

> "As you have heard that the anti-Christ is coming" . . . Therefore when the Lord was asked for a sign of his coming, he began to speak of that coming which can be imitated in signs and wonders by the opposing body.[19]

If one follows the logic of the inner mystery of the union of Head and Body, then the puzzling and contradictory statements in the biblical text can be correctly interpreted under the grace of God.[20]

2. *Of the Lord's Bipartite Body*

The second rule concerns a further aspect of the mystery of the union of Christ and His Body the Church. It is the mystery of the union of all the baptized in "One Body."

---

[18] LR 4:20-23. Froehlich, *Biblical Interpretation*, 107.

[19] LR 5:1-5. Froehlich, *Biblical Interpretation*, 107. John 2:18.

[20] LR 4:22.

There is but one body and one Spirit . . . One Lord, one faith, one baptism (Eph 4:4, 5).

Tyconius draws attention to contradictory prophecies directed at the same Body.

> When the Lord says to the one body, "Invisible treasures I will open up for you that you may know that I am the Lord, and I will adopt you," and then continues, "but you did not recognize me, that I am God, and there is no God beside me, and you did not know me,"[21] do the two statements, though they are addressed to one body actually refer to the same entity, "Invisible treasures I will open up for you that you may recognize that I am God, for the sake of my servant Jacob," and, "But you did not recognize me," and "you did not know me?" "You do not know can only be said to someone who now does know, but "you did not recognize" is addressed to someone who though he should have recognized (God) and seems to belong to the same body, "draws near to God with his lips only, while his heart is far from him."[22] To such a person God can say, "But you did not recognize me."[23]

Tyconius instances Isaiah 42:16,17 where the Lord promises to lead the people on a journey and promises never to forsake them; then they turn back! He lists further contradictions: "chosen," yet "not chosen";[24]

---

[21]Isa 45:3-4.

[22]Isa 29:13.

[23]LR 8:11-24. Frochlich, *Biblical Interpretation*, 111.

[24]Isa 43:27-44:1.

"exalted" and "rebellious" at the one time;[25] Jerusalem, "enriched" and "impoverished"[26] in the same context.

Tyconius argues that these apparent contradictions are resolved when one recognizes the inherent mystery to which the biblical text is conformed, the bipartite nature of the Church.

> . . . that the Body of Christ is bipartite is shown in this brief sentence, "I am dark and beautiful."[27] I cannot think for a moment that the Church "without spot or wrinkle"[28] whom the Lord "cleansed for Himself by His Blood[29] should be "dark" anywhere except on her left side "by which the name of God is blasphemed among the Gentiles."[30] . . . Therefore all the statements throughout Scripture in which God announces that Israel will perish deservedly or that his inheritance will be cursed must be understood in terms of this mystery.[31]

This "rule" concerning the mystery of the bipartite nature of the Church is a central feature of Tyconius' ecclesiology. It is because of his in-

---

[25]Isa 63:9, 10.

[26]Isa 33:20, 23.

[27] Cant 1:5.

[28]Eph 5:27.

[29]Titus 2:14.

[30]Rom 2:24.

[31]LR 10:13 - 11:14. Froehlich, *Biblical Interpretation*, 112, 113.

sistence on this mysterious unity of saint and sinner alike in the "one Body" (Eph 4:4) that his teaching was rejected in Donatist circles.

3. Of Promises and the Law

The third "rule" concerns a different aspect of the mystery of the "one Body" of Christ (Eph 4:4). It concerns the "one hope given to all of you by your call" (Eph 4:5). How was it possible that those who lived "under the Law" were justified?

Tyconius introduces Rule III with as provocative an example of authoritative contradictions as any posed by Abelard in his *Sic et Non!*

> Divine authority tells us that no one has ever been able to achieve justification by works of the law. The same authority asserts in the strongest terms that there have always been people who kept the law and were justified.[32]

It is this "scandal" of contradiction in the sacred text that alerts the exegete to seek the underlying hermeneutical principle which resolves the apparent contradiction. The principle is that the referent of the text may be to either of two "orders," the sons of promise or the sons of law. The first "order" is that of the heirs of Abraham to whom God addresses the promise of life; the second "order" is that of the sons of the law who receive the promise conditionally.

> . . . Rather than impinging on each other, each of the two preserved its own order. For just as the law never hindered faith, so faith never destroyed the law. We read, "Do we therefore through faith

---

[32]LR 12:1-3. Froehlich, *Biblical Interpretation*, 114.

destroy the law? By no means! Rather we establish the law" (Rom 3:31) that is, we strengthen it, for the two strengthen each other.[33]

Tyconius explains that the Promise stands without condition. "The apostle states that the law, given 430 years later neither impeded nor annulled the promise" (Gal 3:17). In his discussion, Tyconius introduces the question of the divine preknowledge and the human free will.

God obviously knew beforehand whether those whom he promised to Abraham would exist of their own free will or not. There are two options: Either they would; in this case, the question is settled. Or they would not; in this case, the God who gave the promise did not keep his word. If it was God's decision to give the promised (nations) if and when they were willing, God certainly would have said so in order to prevent games being played on his servant, Abraham, who believed that "What God has promised, he is able to do" Rom 4:21. God's promise would not be firm, nor would faith retain its integrity. For how could God's promise or Abraham's faith remain stable if that which was promised and believed depended upon the choice of the promised ones? God would have been promising something that was not his, and Abraham would have believed incautiously.[34]

In face of the strength of the divine promises, to whom are conditions addressed?

---

[33]LR 14:7-12. Froehlich, *Biblical Interpretation*, 116.

[34]LR 22:19-30. Froehlich, *Biblical Interpretation*, 124.

But we also encounter conditions, for instance, "If you listen to me and are willing" (Isa 1:19). Where is God's foreknowledge, where is his firm promise in such conditions?[35] . . . The condition, that is, the law, was given for the impious and sinners only (cf. I Tim 1:9) so that they might either flee to grace or receive punishment more justly if they robbed grace of its effect.[36]

The exegete may discern the true referent, one still under the law, rather than one alive in the Spirit,[37] when the prophetic text limits the promise by a condition.

There is great need for careful discernment. Where in Rule II, the contradictory prophetic statements were explained by the bipartite nature of the Church, in Rule III Tyconius warns:

Lest someone thinks, however, that the separation of the two people is so clear, it was arranged for both to exist in one body, in Jacob, who was called both "beloved" and "cheater of his brother."[38]

In a certain sense, both "orders" are addressed by the conditioned "if."

True, even the righteous "whom God foreknew"(Rom 8:20) live under this law. They also are addressed by these words, "if you hear me," but for a different reason; not because they may choose not to

---

[35]LR 24:7-9. Froehlich, *Biblical Interpretation*, 125.

[36]LR 24:18-20. Froehlich, *Biblical Interpretation*, 126.

[37]LR 21:13. Froehlich, *Biblical Interpretation*, 122.

[38]LR 28:23-25. Froehlich, *Biblical Interpretation*, 130.

hear, but so that they may always be solicitous for their salvation, since they do not know their end. Indeed, no one is certain of belonging to the number of the foreknown; even the Apostle is concerned "lest I myself be rejected" (1 Cor 9:27).[39]

Augustine, in his summary of the *Book of Rules* in the *De Doctrina Christiana,* objected that Rule III was not a rule at all but a "great question."[40] However, in Tyconius' categories, it is a "rule" because it introduced a different aspect of the mystery of the bipartite Church. The particular mystery in Rule III concerns the continuing role of Promise and Law in the bipartite Church. There have always been two "orders," two seeds of Abraham in the "One Body," one under Law and one under Promise. This mystery is announced in Jacob, "the one body" who was called both "beloved" and "cheater" of his brother.[41] Through the "logic" of this rule, Tyconius claims that since Israel formed "two orders," under Promise and Law, the Church in its bipartite nature is still under Law and under Promise. The conditions or threats are addressed to the evil members of the Church, while the promise of eternal life itself remains untrammeled by human infidelity.

4. *Of Species and Genus*

Rule IV has a double purpose. It concerns the mystery of the prophetic texts which promise salvation to, or which threaten destruction upon, certain peoples, lands or cities. Tyconius explains that the same city

---

[39]LR 25:25-30. Froehlich, *Biblical Interpretation*, 127.

[40] Augustine, *De Doctrina Christiana* III, 30.

[41]LR 28:35.

can be praiseworthy or blameworthy because it is a "type" of the bipartite Church. Tyre is bipartite,[42] Egypt is bipartite.[43] Tyconius' use of typology is significantly different from Cyprian's. Where Cyprian's typology is Christological,[44] Tyconius uses typology ecclesiologically. Tyconius draws attention to a special problem in typological interpretation, the problem of the historical and the a-historical elements in prophecy. How is the interpreter to explain the exaggerations in the prophetic material that strain the credibility of the text?

Tyconius illustrates this problem in Jeremiah 25.

"Thus says the Lord God of Israel, Take the cup of pure wine from my hands, give it to drink to all the nations to which I send you . . . Jerusalem and the cities of Judah . . . Pharoah, the king of Egypt . . . the kings of all the foreign lands, Ashdod, Gaza, Epron, Edom, Moab – Tyre – Sidon – Dedam – Tema – Buz – Elam, Persia . . ."[45]

Tyconius queries:

Does Jeremiah, when he was in the body, who was taken from Judea, yet never incarcerated except in Egypt, prophesy that pure

---

[42]LR 46:13.

[43]LR 43:1.

[44]M. Fahey, *Cyrian and the Bible: A Study in Third-Century Exegesis* (Tubingen: J.C.B. Mohr, 1971) 623-627.

[45]Jer 25:15-29.

wine openly put into a cup is given as a drink to all the nations which are under heaven, or outside the Church?[46]

The improbability of Jeremiah's being able to fulfill such a command alerts the interpreter of Scripture to apply the prophetic warning not to the cities and lands named in the text but, more universally, to the "opposing body" of Satan throughout the Church. It is this kind of non-literal, a-historical mode of prophecy that Tyconius terms "genus," rather than "species," because of its more immediate application beyond a particular person or place in the biblical text.

At the beginning of his treatment of the topic, Tyconius warns the reader that his use of these terms is different from that of secular usage.

> We are speaking now about species and genus, not according to the rhetorical skill of human wisdom which he who is more able than anyone to speak did not speak "lest he make the cross of Christ empty of meaning," as if, like a falsehood, it should need an aid or an ornamentation.[47]

"Species" prophecies are certain historical events, like the Babylonian captivity[48] or certain individuals, like Solomon,[49] or places, like the cities and towns addressed in the prophetic texts. In dealing with what he calls "species" type prophecy, Tyconius uses the more familiar term

---

[46]LR 54:14-17. Anderson, *Book of Rules*, 146.

[47]LR 31:7-10. Anderson, *Book of Rules*, 97.

[48]LR 39:25-29. Anderson, *Book of Rules*, 117.

[49]LR 39:17. Anderson, *Book of Rules*, 116.

figura. Here in Rule IV, for the first time in the *Book of Rules*, we meet typology,[50] the dominant form of biblical interpretation of the North African
tradition.

> For it is more necessary to know that all the cities or provinces of
> Israel and of the Gentiles which Scripture speaks about or in which
> it refers to some act are a type of the Church; *figuram esse*
> *Ecclesiae,* indeed some types are of the evil kind, some of the good,
> but some are of both kinds.[51]

He identifies Sodom as an evil species,[52] while Solomon,[53]
Nineveh and Egypt[54] are bipartite, that is, a mixture of good and evil.

A "genus" text is that class of prophecy in which the extremity of
its language and imagery militate against its literal application. In other
words, readers should refrain from struggling to justify the historical truth of
the text, and focus their attention immediately on the universal meaning to
which the prophecy is directed, that is, it is directed at the Church. If
Solomon were promised merely a throne it would have been a "species"

---

[50]In his study of Cyprian's exegesis, Michale Fahey adds a short
excursus giving a lexicographical survey of the words Cyprian uses to
express figures and types. Among the common substantives and verbs are:
sacramentum (mysterium); imago; umbra (and their counterparts *veritas* or
*res) figura, exemplum; similituds; praefigurare; praeformae; praecurrere;
significare; exprimere; portare; adimpleri.* Fahey, *Cyprian and the Bible,*
612-622.

[51]LR 39:27. Anderson, *Book of Rules,* 117.

[52]LR 39:28.

[53]LR 38:31.

[54]LR 43:1.

prophecy, in which Solomon is a *figura* or type of the kingship of Christ, but when in 2 Samuel 7:12-16, he is promised an eternal throne, then this is a problem for the reader. Tyconius urges that the loss of the historical kingship in Judea should not raise doubts about the fulfillment of prophetic promises[55] when the language of the text (as in "eternal throne") strains credibility; this is a "key" or signal that the prophecy is directed immediately at the Church.

Both "species" and "genus" prophecies have a double function. The "species" prophecy is double in its referent, in that the prophecy is directed immediately to the individual or city named, and also to its "anti-type" in the life of the Church.[56] On the other hand, the genus, too, has a double function, its hyperbolic tone points to the cataclysms of the "last days,"[57] but also to the judgment already passed on the "nations of wickedness" within the bipartite Church. In this way, Tyconius introduces a complex "backwards and forwards" view of the prophetic text,[58] which respects the literal, historical truth of the biblical text, acknowledges the eschatological dynamic of prophecy, and yet at the same time directs the focus of interpretation to the life of the Church, where the prophesies are fulfilled "spiritually." Rule IV introduces the term spiritaliter (Rev 11:8). In Rule I Tyconius had warned that the coming of the Church (its growth through baptism) was in invisible glory,[59] rather than the manifest glory of the second coming of Christ. In

---

[55]LR 37:24.

[56]In this sense the species is a "part of the whole."

[57]See Jer 25, LR 54. Anderson, *Book of Rules*, 145-6.

[58]"Forwards," from type to antitype; "backwards" from final resurrection to "first resurrection."

[59]LR 4:22.

the same way, the destruction and the curses are already fulfilled in the Church, but "spiritually." The "spiritual deaths" will be manifest in the separation of the bipartite Church at the Judgment.

Speaking of the problem of the historical truth of a "species" prophecy concerning the destruction of Tyre, Tyconius warns of the intricate mixture of "species" and "genus" prophecies in a single passage:

> Is it conceivable that all the kingdoms of every land have reason to come to Tyre to transact business – if Tyre is not the Church in which the whole world has dealings for eternal life?[60]

Concluding his study of the prophecies relating to Tyre, he adds:

> Even if some of these things are clearly seen to have happened already, nevertheless, all things are spiritual.[61]

What Tyconius meant by "species" and "genus" has been explained otherwise. It has been suggested that "species" prophecy, as typology, is directed at the life of the Church, while "genus" prophecy concerns the eschatological realities.[62] This interpretation is problematic because of the clear insistence of Tyconius that the genus prophecies, too, are directed to the Church in its ongoing struggle with the forces of evil.

A clear example of a "genus" prophecy pointing to the Church is the famous passage of the valley of the dry bones in Ezekiel:

---

[60]LR 46:20-23. Anderson, *Book of Rules,* 132.

[61]LR 48:1-2. Anderson, *Book of Rules*, 134.

[62]Anderson, *Book of Rules*, 97-99, footnote 1.

Also, for example, here in the final resurrection the first resurrection is signified. It says "The Lord spoke to me, saying, 'Son of man, these bones are the whole house of Israel. They say, our bones are made dry, our hope has died, we have expired. Therefore, prophesy and say, Thus says the Lord, Behold, I will open your graves and I will bring you out of your graves and I will lead you into the land of Israel, and you will know that I am the Lord when I open your sepulchers and bring my people out of the graves and I will place my spirit in you and you will live and I will place you over your own land and you will know that I am the Lord.'"[63]

The powerful imagery is clearly to be classified as a genus prophecy by Tyconius and is immediately interpreted in an ecclesiological context:

Shall we know the Lord only when we have been clearly resurrected, and not now when we arise through baptism? Either the dead are able to say "Our bones are made dry," or we believe it is promised to the dead deservedly. For God explained that it is in the sacrament, lest it become ambiguous. For we believe that no Christian is doubtful about the final resurrection of the flesh.[64]

---

[63]LR 36:12-21. Anderson, *Book of Rules*,110. Ezek 37:11-14.

[64]LR 36:21-27. Anderson, *Book of Rules*, 110. In his treatise, "On the Resurrection of the Flesh," Tertullian had argued against Gnostic-type allegorizing of the text, and had insisted upon the literal interpretation of the prophecies of the resurrection of the body. In proposing a "spiritual" interpretation, Tyconius had no doubt to take into account the authority of Tertullian in the African Church.

This double referent, first to the "spiritual" resurrection in the Church, and second to the final resurrection, is also present in the Johannine passage:

> "Truly I say to you that he who hears my word and believes him who sent me has eternal life, and he does not come into judgement, but passes to eternal life. . . . Do not be angered by this, because the hour is coming in which all who are in the graves will hear the voice of the Son of God . . ." First he said, "The dead who would hear will live," then second "all who are in the grave will come out."[65]

Rules I, II, and III had concentrated on the mystery of the unity of Christ and the Church, and the mystery of the unity of the "one Body," but bipartite in its nature and destiny; however, in Rule IV, Tyconius introduces another mystery of the nature of the Church. The prophecies that promise salvation or threaten destruction are already being fulfilled "spiritually" in the midst of the bipartite Church.

5. *Of Times*

Rule V not only demonstrates the fascination that numbers, patterns and symbols held for the ancient world, but it concerns the very real problems for the scriptural exegete posed by the interpretation of lengths of time in the biblical texts.

The long and ingenious section on the computation of the three days in the tomb[66] reveals Tyconius' masterly assurance in this area, but his en-

---

[65]LR 36:29 36: 10. Anderson, *Book of Rules,* 111. John 5:24-29. See also LR 37:23-25; 46:20-24.

[66]LR 56:20 - 59:14. Anderson, *Book of Rules,* 151-159.

thusiasm for minute detail does not deflect him from the primary purpose of the Rule which is to show the ecclesial significance of prophetic numbers.

The discussion centers on the problem of interpreting the "quantity of time" *temporis quantitas* (LR 55:1) in Scripture. For Tyconius, the meaning of the biblical numbers is clear if you follow the inner logic of the mystery of biblical "times."

There are two kinds of "times." First, those in which perplexities are resolved by the "mystical trope, synecdoche."[67] This method resolves the apparent contradictions in the text by taking a part for the whole, or the whole for the part. This is the method Tyconius employs for the problem of literal truth of the three days of Christ's burial.

The second of these "time quantities" he calls *legitimis numeris* "legitimate" or "fixed" numbers (LR 55:2). They are time quantities "fixed" or "legitimated" by the inner logic of the Law. These are not literal time quantities but indicators that the passage is to be "spiritually" interpreted, that is, interpreted in the context of the Church. Sevens, tens, twelves and their multiples are such indicators. These indicators, like the "70 years" in Babylon, the "ten days"[68] of the Book of Revelation are not definite quantitative periods, but indications of the "whole time" – the time of the Church.

---

[67]LR 55:1-4. Anderson, *Book of Rules*, 148. Quintilian, *Institutio Oratioria,* viii 6. 19: "*Synecdoche* has the power to give variety to our language by making us realize many things from one, the whole from a part" (transl. H.E. Butler, The Loeb Classical Library) 311.

[68]Rev 2:10.

The whole is understood from the part, because a certain time is defined by legitimate numbers, as in the Revelations "you will have
tribulations for ten days" when it means "until the end."[69]

He makes a number of references to this "whole time" which is the
time of the Church; of particular significance to the millenarian debate is his
insistence of the spiritual interpretation of the number one thousand, which is
the "whole time" of the first resurrection – that is, the "resurrection" of sinful
humanity through baptism in the Church.

A further example of the symbolic use of numbers is found in
phrases like "the last *hour*," "the *day* of salvation," "the acceptable *year* of the
Lord."[70] These are not to be interpreted literally, but as prophetic warnings
of the urgency of the call to conversion. Like the "fixed" numbers, they are
indefinite in quantity.

These two devices, first synecdoche, which takes seriously the actual
time quantity but resolves difficulties by taking the part for the whole and
vice versa, and second the indefinite "fixed" numbers or the prophetic phrases
like "today," assist the interpreter in the "obscurity" of biblical numbers.
More importantly, they explain the immediate ecclesiological significance of
those prophetic texts.

The mystery of the interpretation of the "times" of Scripture is an
especially important "rule" for Tyconius. Writing in the fifth century,
Gennadius notes the importance of Tyconius' contribution to biblical interpretation in this respect:

---

[69]LR 60:9. Anderson, *Book of Rules*, 161.

[70]LR 60:20. Anderson, *Book of Rules*, 162.

> In this exposition [the *Apocalypse Commentary*] . . . he [Tyconius] doubts that there will be a reign of the righteous on the earth for a thousand years after the resurrection, so that there will be two resurrections of the dead in the flesh, one of the righteous and one of the unrighteous . . .[71]

For Tyconius, the "logic" of rule "of times" reveals that the "reign of the righteous" of the right side of the Body is already a "spiritual" reality in the Church. This reality is indicated by the key of the "fixed number," one thousand years.

In Rule V the "doubleness" of the Church is reflected in the 'doubleness' of time. Referring to the seven years of fruitfulness that were followed by the seven years of famine (LR 64:8 ff), Tyconius claims that in the Church the "spiritual" fruitfulness and the famine occur simultaneously because of its bipartite nature.

6. On Recapitulation

Rule VI addresses the mystery of signs of the "separation" of the good and the evil that will be effected in the Judgment at the Second Coming. A "recapitulation" occurs when certain events happening in the present time bear a resemblance *similitudines* (LR67:8) to events described in Scripture.

> ...de similitudine itaque tempus suum et nostrum unum
> fecit et iuncxit ... (LR 67:26)
>
> ...thus through a similitude, he made their times and ours
> one and joined them....

---

[71]Gennadius, *Lives of Illustrious Men,* 389.

Tyconius claims that there are two kinds of these "recapitulations," the first is a similitude of happenings in the present with something in the past. The Donatist Church of fourth century Africa suffering the repressions and destruction of life and property under a series of imperial legates may well have felt that their own experience mirrored in some way the evils that surrounded Lot and his family in Sodom (LR 66:17).

A second kind of "recapitulation" occurred when the present situation mirrored a future event. The present sufferings of the Donatist community under the repressions of a Christian emperor were a "likeness of what was to be" *futurae similitudines* (LR 67:11) in the end times foretold by the prophet Daniel.

> "When you see what was said by the prophet Daniel
> then let those who are in Judea flee to the mountains,"
> and he imagines the end of time. But what Daniel said
> is now going on in Africa, and the end is not at this
> time. (LR 67:8-10)

As always in the *Book of Rules*, the attention of the exegete is not focused on the final advent – all too clearly to be manifested; but rather on the discernment of the signs by which true incorporation into the "right" side of the Body of Christ are already to be discerned.

Tyconius warns that these "recapitulations" are particularly obscure:

> Among all the rules by which the Spirit signified the principle with
> which the way of life should be guarded, one in particular guards the
> sign of recapitulation with that principle of subtlety; so that the

continuation of a narrative might be seen more than the recapitulation.[72]

Sometimes the signal of the recapitulation[73] is cryptic phrases like "then," "at that hour":

"At that hour, let him who will be on the roof, and his vessels in the house, not descend to take them away; and let him who is in the field likewise not turn back: remember Lot's wife."[74]

The signal "at that hour," as explained in the previous Rule on "Times," announces that the passage contains a prophetic warning to be heeded *nunc* in the time of the Church. It is an injunction to the Christian to be radically detached from all that would separate us from Christ. The suffer-

---

[72]LR 66:11-14. Anderson, *Book of Rules*, 180.

[73]Scholars have long debated the meaning of "recapitulation" in Rule VI. (Burkitt, *Book of Rules,* xvi, xxxvii; Monceaux, *Histoire Littéraire de l'Afrique Chrétienne,*187). For the "recapitulation" of Eph 1:10, Tyconius supplies the verb, *restaurare* LR 18:27, where Hilary and Augustine use *instaurare*. In Rule VI, Tyconius does not introduce the term *recapitulatio* in the context of Eph 1:10. The theme of the chapter concerns "being with Christ" or "being separated from Christ." Tertullian translates *anakephalaiosasthai* of Eph 1:10 by *recapitulare* in his treatise *Against Marcion* 5:17, and then argues against Marcion's "alien Christ": "Now, if it is impossible for all these things from the beginning to be reckoned to any other God than the Creator, who will believe that an alien god has recapitulated them in an alien Christ, instead of their own proper Author in His own Christ? If, again, they belong to Christ, they must need be separate from the other god; and if separated then opposed to him. But then how can opposites be gathered together into him by whom they are in short destroyed?" *Latin Christianity: Its Founder* Tertullian (The Ante Nicene Fathers; Grand Rapids, Michigan: W. Eerdmans, 1963) 465.

[74]Luke 17:31-32.

ings and persecutions the Church is now enduring in Africa[75] are a similitude
of the end times. The signs of who are being gathered to Christ, and who are
separating themselves from Christ, are already to be discerned by careful
attention to the prophetic texts.

> For if he loves God, let him explain this by his deeds, let him ad-
> here to God, let him love God in his brother. If he believes that
> Christ became incarnate, let him cease to hate the members of
> Christ.[76]

Neither the Donatist party with their apocalyptic-style vision of a
pure remnant awaiting the vindication of the end-times, nor the Catholic
party, their orthodoxy bolstered up by imperial forces, could take much con-
solation from such arguments. The fervor of such writing shows how the
pen of the exegete could be turned to moving exhortation, even while he pursued the logic of his hermeneutical exposition.

Rule VI, "on Recapitulation," is concerned with that area of
eschatological expectation so important to the early Church, the discernment
of the "signs of the times." While not denying that the end is approaching,
Tyconius insists that the interpreter is to recognize the signs of the separation
of the two parts of the one Body, the Church, already manifest in the deeds of
love or of hate within the membership of the Church.

---

[75]LR 67:11. The Donatist Church of Africa had suffered repression
under a series of imperial legates from the early years of the fourth century.
There were only short respites in a century of general upheaval and unrest.
Frend examines the complex social, political and religious causes in his
history of the Donatist Church. (See Chapter Four.) The devastations, the
killings in the "name of Christ" are pictures, "similitudes" of the end times.

[76]LR 68:16-19. Anderson, *Book of Rules*, 186-7.

7. *Of the Devil and His Body*

Rule VII introduces the mystery of the revelation of the Antichrist, (2 Thess 2:7), another area of special concern for the exegetes of the early Church, when the "mystery of iniquity" will seek to be enthroned in the temple (2 Thess 2:4).

Tyconius concentrates on two prophetic texts Isaiah 14:12-21 against the King of Babylon and Ezekiel 28:2-19 against the Prince of Tyre. In particular he draws attention to the absurdity of the Lucifer's aspiration in the Isaian prophecy.

> How Lucifer rising early fell from Heaven: He is bowed down on earth who sent to all the nations! However you said in your mind: I will ascend to heaven; above the stars of God I will place my throne, I will sit on a mountain high above the high mountains in the north; I will ascend above the clouds, I will be like the most High . . .[77]

Tyconius remarks that the impossibility of such an aspiration is a signal within the text that the interpreter must seek a deeper meaning.

> . . .besides the reason that neither the devil nor man can hope that he himself is able to ascend to heaven, and sitting above the stars make himself into God, the same Scripture also warns that a deeper inquiry must be made *aliud inquirendum admonet*.[78]

---

[77]Isa 14:12-21.

[78]LR 71:15-18. Anderson, *Book of Rules*, 195.

The spiritual interpretation is that "heaven" in the prophetic text is the "Church," and the ambition of the "mystery of iniquity" is to be enthroned in this very Temple of God.[79] The task of the exegete is to clarify this prophetic warning for the Church, so that there is an awareness of the growth of the power of the "opposing body."[80]

"Lucifer" introduces a complex set of references. In the *Book of Revelation*, Christ is called the "bright star of the morning" *stella splendida matutina*.[81] Satan's title of "Lucifer" underlines his deceptive likeness to Christ.[82] Because of the union of Satan and his "Body," the title "Lucifer," a prophetic text may refer either to Satan or to Antichrist, the "man of sin." Unlike Origen who refers the same prophetic texts (Isa 14 and Ezek 28) to Satan, Tyconius insists that in the context of Isaiah 14, Lucifer refers to Antichrist rather than Satan. Antichrist is human not demonic. Antichrist is a member of the Church. Antichrist is "in the midst" of the Church.

The Isaian text which speaks of the fall of Lucifer from heaven, when interpreted spiritually, refers to those evil members of the Church who have indeed "fallen" from their baptismal union with Christ. This "opposing body" has fallen from Heaven the Church.[83] When the text speaks of Lucifer's ambition to place his throne above the stars, the referent here shifts

---

[79]LR 71:23. Anderson, *Book of Rules*, 96.

[80]Rule I, LR 7:24 - 8:3.

[81]Rev 22:16, 17.

[82]LR 71:28, 29. Anderson, *Book of Rules*, 196.

[83]LR 71:23.

to Satan, the head of the evil body, and to his "great ones," who seek to dominate "the stars of God, that is, the saints."[84]

The prophetic condemnation of such ambitions is clear:

> Thus the Lord says through Obadiah the prophet to this Esau, that is to the evil brothers, "Exalting his dwelling place, saying in his heart, who will bring me down to the earth? Though you should be exalted just as the eagle and place your nest among the stars, thence I will bring you down from these," says the Lord.[85]

Rule VII concerns the revelation of the "mystery of iniquity" (2 Thess 2:7). The "opposing body," the evil members of the bipartite Church, will be revealed at the Day of Judgment when those united with Christ, in the Spirit, will be taken "from the midst," out of that temple doomed to destruction in which Antichrist dared to set up his throne (2 Thess 2:4). However, Tyconius emphasizes that the presence of this "mystery of iniquity" (2 Thess 2:7) is already revealed in the prophetic texts. "You were meant for destruction and you will be no more" (Ezek 28:19).

TYCONIUS AND THE "MYSTERY OF INIQUITY" (2 THESS 2:7)

The chapter has concentrated on the author's stated intention at the beginning of the *Book of Rules* of introducing his readers to a systematic treatment of the problems and obscurities in Scripture in seven specific areas of biblical interpretation. However, it becomes clear as one reads the text that the *Book of Rules* is far from a dispassionate handbook that should prove

---

[84]LR 71:1-14.

[85]Obadiah 3-4.

useful for clearing up obscurities in the text. There is a compelling theological theme throughout the book.

In his commentary on the third rule of Tyconius, Augustine claims that it is not really a hermeneutical rule so much as a "great question."[86] It may be just as true to say that the whole *Book of Rules* is a "great question," and that question is the "mystery of iniquity"[87] in the Church. It is an ecclesiological question, and it helps to explain the paradox that the ecclesiology of Tyconius has interested many of his readers more than his hermeneutics. However, one of the besetting problems in the study of the *Book of Rules* has been neglect of the systematic nature of Tyconius' thought. The double purpose of the *Book of Rules* as an investigation into the obscurities of the prophetic texts and into the "great question" of the presence of evil in the Church, is inextricably linked together.

While the immediate practical purpose of the *Book of Rules* is concerned with problems and obscurities in the interpretation of seven "mysteries" of the prophetic texts, throughout the *Book of Rules* Tyconius has insisted upon the importance of the concept of the bipartite Church. With Cyprian, he insists upon the unity of the one Body throughout the world, but Tyconius brings a new dimension to the question of the unity of the Body, and that is his teaching on the "mystery of iniquity" (2 Thess 2:7) revealed by the prophetic texts.

It is through this prophetic revelation that we come to know the nature of the Church as bipartite, a mixture of good and evil in one body. Tyconius does not enter into the argument between Optatus and Parmenian about how to recognize the features of the true Church (Donatist or Catholic).

---

[86]Augustine *De Doctrina Christiana* III:33.

[87]2 Thess 2:7.

According to Tyconius what one has to recognize in the mysteries of prophecy is the very nature of the Church as "bipartite." At the conclusion of Rule II, "On the Bipartite Body of the Lord," Tyconius draws attention to the mystery of the seven angels of the apocalypse (Rev 1:20 - 3:22). Among the seven are numbered both saints and sinners. This demonstrates the very nature of the bipartite Church. It is sevenfold, *id est Ecclesiam septiformem.*[88]

The *Book of Rules*, then, has a double purpose. First, the immediate purpose of introducing the reader to the inner "logic" of the prophetic text. This is the precise hermeneutical purpose, and second, to explain his theology of the bipartite nature of the Church. However, this theological purpose is linked with his understanding of the task of Christian hermeneutics. The mysteries of Scripture are "opened" by the grace of the Spirit so that the sinful members of the Church may be called to repentance. The task of the Christian interpreter is to keep before the reader of the Scriptures the call to faith and conversion by which the Spirit vivifies "the spiritual world, that is, the Church,"[89] that union of life and love between the Head and the Body.

---

[88]LR 11:3.

[89]LR 61:63.

CHAPTER FOUR

THE LOGICAL STRUCTURE OF THE *BOOK OF RULES*

THE ENIGMA OF THE LITERARY STRUCTURE

The careful reading of the *Book of Rules* makes one increasingly aware of Tyconius' craft as a writer. On the one hand, his is a terse, no-nonsense prose with little attention to the elegance of style and the vivid touches one finds in Ambrose and Augustine. On the other hand, one cannot but be aware of a forceful, logical mind marshalling his arguments with careful strategy.

An appreciation of this ability leads one to question whether there is a logical sequence in the ordering of the topics in the *Book of Rules*. It will be argued that an analysis of the ordering of the seven rules is an indispensable key to the understanding of the hermeneutical theory which underlies the *Book of Rules*.

In the past, there have been strong criticisms levelled at Tyconius' compositional ability. In his introduction to the translation and commentary of the *Book of Rules,* Anderson remarked that while it testified to "a creative, original, devout thinker, the work was not without faults":

> The book is uneven and poorly organized. It would have been more logical for Rules I and VII to have been placed together. There does not seem to be any logic to the topics discussed. . . .[1]

---

[1] Anderson, *Book of Rules,* 17.

Earlier in the century, Monceaux had suggested a three-part division
to make sense of these compositional anomalies:

1. The exposition of the theory, Rules I, II and VII.

2. The demonstration of the theory, Rules IV, V, VI.

3. A "digression," Rule III.

On y distingue: 1º une théorie générale, exposée dans les chapitres
qui correspondent aux deux premières règles et à la dernière; 2º une
méthode pratique d'interprétation, avec exemples à l'appui, méthode
expliquée dans les chapitres relatifs à la quatrième, à la cinquième et
à la sixième règle; 3º la digression qui remplit le troisième chapitre,
et que l'auteur qualifie également de règle. C'est moins une «règle»
proprement dite, que la discussion d'une question préjudicielle: une
sorte d'introduction à l'exégèse de l'Ancien Testament, considéré dans
ses rapports avec la Loi nouvelle.[2]

But for Monceaux the structural difficulties are unresolved, and he
draws attention to the contrast between the problems of the general arrangement of the work and the vigor of Tyconius' thought and the originality of
his doctrine:

On doit reconnaitre que, chez Tyconius, l'art de la composition est
médiocre. Ne parlons pas du *Commentaire sur l'Apocalypse,* ni des
ouvrages de polémique, qu'on ne peut apprécier à cet égard d'après des
fragments, si nombreux qu'ils soient. Mais nous possédons encore,
tout entier, le livre des *Regulæ;* et nous y avons relevé d'assez

---

[2]Monceaux, *Histoire Littéraire de l'Afrique Chrétienne V,* 182.

graves défauts de composition. Incertitude dans le plan d'ensemble: les règles sont de portée très inégale, et l'une au moins est à peine une «règle», et l'ordre de succession ne correspond pas à la logique du système. Manque de proportions entre les parties: les chapitres sont de dimensions très différentes, et de trop longues digressions s'intercalent entre des notes trop sèches. Raideur et monotonie dans la disposition intérieure des chapitres: une brève définition de la règle, puis une interminable série d'exemples, coupée de loin en loin par une observation générale ou une phrase de controverse. Pour tout dire enfin, la mise en œuvre trahit une sorte de maladresse, qui contraste avec la vigueur de la conception et l'originalité de la doctrine.[3]

THE "LOGIC" OF THE LITERARY STRUCTURE

In spite of the criticism that has been levelled at Tyconius' compositional ability, it will be argued that there is a carefully designed literary structure for the *Book of Rules* as a whole. Just as Tyconius had been most anxious that the "logic" of the individual rules be understood, he has provided a literary frame for introducing the "logic" of the theory that underlies the notion of "mystical" rules.

Whether he has been successful in elucidating his notion of "rule" is another question. Augustine's puzzled reaction to the question is an indication of its difficulty. Chapter Five of the present work will concentrate on the Tyconian notion of "rule" and the reasons for Augustine's misreading of this basis concept of Tyconian hermeneutics. At this point in the analysis of

---

[3]Monceaux, *Histoire Littéraire de l'Afrique Chrétienne V*, 210-1. See detailed criticisms, 182.

the *Book of Rules* it will be argued that one of the indispensable steps in understanding what Tyconius meant by the "mystical" rules of Scripture is to examine the literary structure of the work as a whole.

An important key to the understanding of the "logic" of the literary structure of the book is the elaborateness of the preamble to Rule IV, the central chapter of the seven "rules." This preamble (LR 33:7-34) recalls the themes of "obscuring" and revealing in the preamble to the *Book of Rules* itself. These themes are not only recalled but they are deepened when the hermeneutical theory of the "mystical rules" of Scripture in the first preamble are transformed into a theology of the Spirit, the Author of Scripture, who speaks in words of "subtle eloquence" throughout the Scriptures (LR 31:19).

While the importance of Rule IV for the understanding of the notion of "rule" is indicated by the paralleling of themes in both preambles, there are a number of other literary devices that suggest that there was careful structuring of the work as a literary unit.

The linking by title of the first rule, "on the Lord and His Body," and the last rule, "on the Devil and His Body," forms an obvious literary inclusion, but a study of the images and themes that link Rules II and VI and Rules III and V suggest that the *Book of Rules* was conceived in a concentric pattern with Rule IV as the central focus in the development of the hermeneutical theory.

An outline of the structure is suggested below:

The Concentric Structure

      a Rule I   - the images of "stones," "mountains"

      b Rule II   - the theme of "separation"

      c Rule III - the "deceitful" presence of evil

      d Rule IV - a development of the themes from the Prologue

    c' Rule V   - the "deceitful" presence of evil

    b' Rule VI   - the theme of "separation"

    a' Rule VII - the image of "stones" and "mountains"

THE PARALLEL RULES

1. Rules I and VII – "Stones" and "Mountains"

Rule I and Rule VII are explicitly linked in the introduction of Rule VII.

> Diaboli et corporis eius ratio breuiter videri potest, si id quod de Domino et eius corpore dictum est in hoc quoque observetur. transitus namque a capite ad corpus eadem ratione dinoscitur.

> The rule about the devil and his body can be seen briefly if that which was said concerning the Lord and his body is noted here also. For indeed a transition from the head to the body is discerned by this same reason . . .[4]

Besides the author's explicit paralleling of the two rules through topic title, and his references to the same logical transitions of the referent from the head to the body, there are other significant parallels both in images and themes in the treatment of the two topics.

Notable among these parallels is the imagery of the "stone" and the "mountain" as recurring motifs in the prophetic material cited by Tyconius in the Rule I and Rule VII of the *Book of Rules*. A central theme of the whole

---

[4]LR 70:11-13. Anderson, *Book of Rules*, 192.

work, the ongoing conflict[5] between the two opposing bodies, is specifically related to the dominant imagery of "stone" and "mountain" in Rule I and Rule VII.

Rule I is introduced by a brief illustration of the transitions in the prophetic referents from Head to Body in the Isaian text 53: 3-6; 10-11; then the author moves on to Daniel 2: 34-35:

> Daniel also says that "the stone cut from the mountain" both "trampled" upon the body of the kingdom of the world, and that the Lord "ground them into dust" but a mountain was made and its body "filled the whole world."[6]

Both the stone that "grows" and the mountain that "fills the earth" are the Church, the Body of Christ. This introduces the ecclesiological principle of the continual growth of the Church in the birth of its members in baptism[7] and that of the presence of the Church throughout the world.[8] At the same time it announces a second ecclesiological principle, that of the inner conflict in which the Church is engaged. This is explored in Daniel 11:31, 36, 38 which speaks of the "last king" providing as it were a Church

---

[5]See insistence on the present tense, Rule I, LR 7:24-26 ". . .the Son of Man who *comes* daily . . ." and Rule VII, LR 75:15, 16 "Here is the man who *shakes* the earth . . . ."

[6]LR 2:15-18. Anderson, *Book of Rules*, 27.

[7]Rule I, LR 4:25-30.

[8]This is contrary to Donatist teaching. Note Augustine's comment at the beginning of his summary of the Rules: "A certain Tyconius, who, although a Donatist, has written most triumphantly against the Donatists . . ." *De Doctrina Christiana*, III, 30.

in the place of the Church – *veluti Ecclesiam in loco Ecclesiae,* an "abomination of desolation in the holy place."[9]

Tyconius concludes the discussion of Rule I with a final reference to the "daily" coming to birth of the Church and its "growth" into the holy temple of God":[10]

> Corpus itaque in capite suo filius est Dei, et Deus in corpore suo filius est hominis, qui cotidie nascendo venit et crescit in templum sanctum Dei. (LR 7:26)

> In its Head, therefore, the Body is the Son of God, and in His Body, God is the Son of Man who comes daily through a birth and grows into God's holy temple.[11]

But he reminds the reader that the temple is bipartite:

> templum enim bipertitum est, cuius pars alterna quamvis lapidibus magis extruatur destruitur, neque in eo lapis super lapidem relinquitur. (LR 7:26 8:2)

> for the temple is bipartite, each part of which is being destroyed, although it is built out of great stones, and in it, "a stone will not be left upon a stone."[12]

---

[9]LR 5:22-4. cf. Matt 24:15.

[10]Gal 3:28, 29.

[11]Froelich, *Biblical Interpretation*, 110.

[12]LR 7:26, 27. Eph 2:2, Matt 24:2.

The whole of Rule VII is organized around the exegesis of two texts, the first, Isaiah 14:12-21, addressed to the king of Babylon[13] and the second, Ezekiel 28: 2-19, addressed to the king of Tyre.[14]

The first text pictures an enthronement of evil "on a mountain high above the high mountains of the north."[15] The discussion of Rule I had established that the Church was imaged as a mountain in Daniel 2:34-35, and now in Rule VII Tyconius refers back to this earlier imagery[16] in opposing this "mountain of God," Mount Sion, where God has set His throne, to the mountain of the devil's enthronement.

While Tyconius introduces a favorite Donatist theme, the kingdoms of the North and South, again he parts company with other Donatist exegetes in refusing the referents to a true and false Church, the true Church of the Donatists in the Numidian South and the Catholic party to the North. Tyconius insists that both the evil mountain of the North and the holy mountain of the South are to be found throughout the world. This is consistent both with his hermeneutical method of the "spiritual" interpretation and with his ecclesiology in which both good and evil are found throughout the Church, "both parts are throughout the world."[17]

The Ezekiel passage takes up the theme of the presence of evil in the Church in another set of images. Here Ezekiel pictures the "Prince of Tyre" aspiring to place his throne "in the heart of the sea."

---

[13]LR 70:14 - 77:14.

[14]LR 77:15 - 85:27.

[15]LR 70:18.

[16]LR 73:8. Joel 3:17.

[17]LR 75:5, 6.

Because your heart is exalted and you have said, "I am God, I dwelled in the dwelling place of God in the heart of the sea." But you are a man and not God . . .[18]

This text goes on to speak of the "precious stones" and the treasures of the king of Tyre.

Thus says the Lord, you are a sign of likeness[19] and a crown of beauty have you been in the pleasures of the paradise of God, having bound to yourself every precious stone, sardius, topaz, emerald and carbuncle and sapphire and jasper and silver and gold and ligurius and agate and amethyst and chrysolite and beryl and onyx -- and with gold you replenished your treasures and your storehouses . . . I placed you along with cherubim on the holy mountain of God, you were in the midst of the stones of fire . . .[20]

The "precious stones" are those gifted members of the Church stolen from God by the devil, and Tyconius notes that they are twelve in number,[21] paralleling the twelve stones of the City of God,[22] but the "precious stones"

---

[18]Ezek 28:2.

[19]For Tyconius this "sign of likeness" is a sure indication that the prophetic text is referring to the Antichrist who mimics the signs and attributes of the Body of Christ.

[20]LR 78:1-14. Anderson, *Book of Rules*, 212.

[21]LR 81:29.

[22]LR 82:5.

of the devil are inferior in substance to the "stones of fire" – "that is the holy men who together make up the mountain of God."[23]

> And you, brethren, as living stones be built up for a spiritual house.[24]

Rule VII concludes with the promise that, like Lot from the burning ruins of Sodom, the Church will be saved from the destruction to which the devil and his body are destined.[25]

The parallels, then, between Rule I and Rule VII are established (a) by explicit reference at the beginning of Rule VII by the common themes of the union of Head and members and (b) by the recurring images of "stones" and "mountains."

2. Rules II and VI – the theme of "separation"

Both Rule II and Rule VI are concerned with the "separateness" of the right and the left side of the "bipartite" Church.

The argument of Rule II is concerned with more than the exegetical problems of discerning the correct referent in the biblical texts which speak of salvation and condemnation; it is also an admonition to the Church of the "separation" of the guilty members. In his discussion of the words of the Canticle "I am dark and beautiful"[26] Tyconius notes:

---

[23]LR 83:10, 11. Anderson, *Book of Rules,* 227.

[24]LR 83:16.

[25]LR 85. Anderson, *Book of Rules,* 232-4.

[26]Cant 1:5

In the same mysterious fashion the Lord mentions seven angels in the Book of Revelation, pointing to a seven-fold Church; sometimes its members are saints and keepers of the commandments, sometimes they are guilty of numerous sins and need to repent. In the Gospel, he attributes various kinds of merit to one body of stewards, saying first: "Blessed is that servant when his master, when he comes, shall find so doing," but continuing about the same person: *denique non totum sed partem eius cum hypocritis ponet*", "but when that wicked servant . . ." and adding: "The Lord will divide him in two parts." I ask, will the Lord divide or cut him up as a whole? Note the final statement: "He will give him apart" – not the whole! – "with the hypocrites."[27]

This theme of the "separation" of the unjust and the gathering of the just to the Lord is the dominant theme of Rule VI which Tyconius entitles the "Recapitulation." Tyconius insists that there is to be no manifest "separation" of the "wheat and the chaff"[28] until the Second Coming of Christ. The mysterious intermingling of good and evil in the Church will

---

[27]LR 11:1-11. Froehlich, *Biblical Interpretation*, 113. Matt 24:48, 51.

[28]Matt 13:30. Optatus, the Catholic bishop opposing Tyconius' Donatist bishop, Parmenian, had also insisted on this point. "In like manner, Christ has commanded that both His own seeds, and those which belong to the other, should grow in His field throughout the entire world, in which there is the one Church. . . . So it is our declaration that we do not reject you. For it would be a sin for us Bishops to do now, that which was not done by the Apostles, who were not permitted either to separate seeds or to pluck up the tares from the wheat." O. R. Vassall-Phillips, *The Work of Optatus Bishop of Milevis: Against the Donatists* (London: Longmans & Co., 1917) 282-283.

continue until the glorious coming of the Lord, gathering to Himself the pu-
rified Church.

Then to what "separations" do the "recapitulations" in the prophetic
text point? The devastations and the human miseries prophesied by Daniel
are all around them as Christian persecutes Christian in fourth century
Africa.[29]

> But what Daniel said is going on now in Africa, and the end is not
> at this time.[30]

The urgent pastoral task of the Christian exegete is to discern the
signs of that "separation" that is already occuring in the Church throughout
the world,[31] of those whose deeds show them to be "separate from Jesus,"[32]
even though they may continue to proclaim their allegiance to Christ.[33]

---

[29]Frend describes the repressions of the Donatists after the accession
of Valentinian and Valens in October 364. "Whatever leanings the Emperors
may have felt towards the Arians of the West, they had no sympathy for the
Donatists. In the *Comes Africae*, Romanus, the latter found an enemy who
was prepared once more to restore Catholicism with the aid of the troops
under his command. . . For the poor, extortion and corrupt administration
were added to the hardships caused by the renewed period of repression and
insecurity. Few imperial representatives in Africa left so evil a name as
Count Romanus." Frend, *The Donatist Church*, 197.

[30]LR 67:8-10.

[31]LR 67:14.

[32]1 John 4:1-3 LR 68:2 *qui soluit Iesum.* The Greek text of 1 John
4:3 of the Aland edition reads *kai pan pneuma ho me homologei ton Jesoun,*
but notes the "italic" variant *kai pan pneuma Iuei ton Jesoun. The Greek
New Testament,* ed. Kurt Aland, Mathew Black, Carlo Martini, Bruce
Metzger, Allen Wikgren 2nd edition (New York: American Bible Society,
1966).

[33]LR 68:13.

"Wheat and chaff" may grow together till the harvest, but already the prophetic texts and their interpreters are revealing the "man of sin."[34]

Tyconius turns to the text of the first letter of John.

> "Many false prophets have gone out into this world. By this you know the Spirit of God: Every spirit which is separate from Jesus and denies that he came in the flesh is not from God, but this is not from God, but this one is from Antichrist, which you heard is coming and is now present in this world."[35] Does anyone have the Spirit of God who denies that Jesus has come in the flesh? But in every way this same epistle, in which he wrote only about good and evil brethren, warns by this same type of speaking that this denial is indeed, not in word, and that each person ought to be known not by what he says, but by his fruits, just as it says, "By this we know that we know him, if we keep his precepts. But he who says that he knows him, and does not keep his precepts is a liar."[36]

The clearest sign of being "separate from Jesus" is hatred of the members of the Body of Christ. Tyconius asks if the one professing to be a Christian "believes that the Word was made flesh, why does he persecute the Word in the flesh? . . . there is not another greater and more evident sign for knowing the Antichrist than that one denies Christ in the flesh, that is, one hates his brother."[37]

---

[34] 2 Thess 2:3.

[35] 1 John 4:1-3.

[36] 1 John 2:3-4. LR 67:31 - 68:12.

[37] LR 68:13.

The careful discernment of the transitions of the referents in the biblical text between the "left" and "right" in the Church (Rule II), and the equally careful discernment of the prophetic signs of those "separate from Jesus" and those united in the one spirit with their Lord (Rule VI) forge the links between the two rules.

The attention is focused upon the polarities between the two opposing bodies. In Rule II, Tyconius points to the polarities in the destiny that awaits them – for the right, the promised salvation, for the left, the threatened condemnation. Rule VI concentrates on the signs that distinguish the two bodies – the one persecuting the members of Christ, the other professing the Lordship of Christ in deeds of love.

3. Rules III and Rule V, the deceitful presence of evil

It has been argued that the two pairs of rules considered so far, I and VII; II and VI, have focused on different aspects of the mystery of the Church.

In Rules I and VII, the universality of the Church was stressed, not only in the positive aspect of its spread throughout the nations,[38] but also in the negative aspect of the mystery of the mixture of good and evil throughout

---

[38]Daniel 2:34-35. LR 2:30. et crescendo terram omnem texit. In *The Unity of the Church,* 5, Cyprian speaks of the unity of the Church throughout the world. "Thus, too, the Church bathed in the light of the Lord projects its rays over the whole world, yet there is one light which is diffused everywhere, and the unity of the body is not separated. She extends here branches over the whole earth in fruitful abundance, she extends her richly flowing streams far and wide; yet her head is one, and her source is one. . ." *Saint Cyprian: Treatises,* trans. and ed., R. J. Deferrari (New York: Fathers of the Church, Inc., 1958) 100.

the whole body.[39] Rule I had concluded with the warning for watchful attention to be paid to the continuing "advent" of evil in the Church.[40]

In Rules II and VI, the emphasis moves beyond an awareness of the presence of this mixture of good and evil in the Church to the principles of the discernment of the "separations," the distinctions between the two opposing groups in the one body.

There is an increasing degree of subtlety in the hermeneutical task. In this respect Rules III and V represent a further refining process, as the structured argument moves toward the center of the symmetrical arrangement of the seven rules.

In both III and V, the radical opposition between the two parts of the Church is once again affirmed, but Tyconius warns of the great need for careful discernment:

> In quam vero partem lex proprie conveniat, licet uni detur corpori, Dominus in Evangelio declarat dicens apostolis: 'Si haec scitis beati estis si feceritis ea. non de omnibus vobis dico; ego scio quos elegi.' magna brevitas ostendentis unum corpus et separantis!

> But to which part of the body the law properly applies, although it may be given to one body, the Lord declares in the Gospel, saying to the apostles: "If you know these things blessed are you if you do them. I am not speaking about all of you; I know whom I have

---

[39]Matt 13:30. The wheat and the tares growing together until the harvest. Optatus in his treatise against the Donatists insisted that the wheat and the tares "should grow throughout the entire world, in which there is the One Church." *Optatus of Milevis*, 282.

[40]LR 8:1-3.

chosen." What great brevity in showing and in separating the one body . . . [41]

While the ongoing opposition is affirmed, yet the subtlety of the argument in Rules III and V warns against any simplistic application of the hermeneutical principles discussed in Rule II or Rule VI, especially any division of the membership of the Church into a "Church of the saved" and a "Church of the reprobate," as Tyconius' fellow Donatists would argue.

Rule III is a nuanced investigation into the Pauline theme of the relationship between Law and Promise, in the context of the image of the double seed of Abraham. The double seed of Abraham, one spiritual and a son of promise, the other carnal and a son of law, forms two continuing "orders"[42] in the life of the Church. This mystery is imaged in Jacob, whose bipartite nature is alluded to in the prophetic text:

> "In the womb he supplanted his brother and in his labours he prevailed against God, and he prevailed with the angel and he became powerful."[43] For the figure is of a two-fold seed of Abraham, that is, of two people struggling in the one womb of mother Church.[44]

Referring again to Jacob in his deceitful reception of his father's blessing, Tyconius notes:

---

[41]LR 26:5-9. Anderson, *Book of Rules*, 83.

[42]LR 14:8.

[43]Hosea 12:2-4.

[44]LR 28:12-8. Anderson, *Book of Rules*, 89. Gen 25:23.

However Jacob, that is, the Church, never came for the blessing un-
accompanied by deceit, that is, by false brothers. But it is not that
innocence and deceit came at the same time for the blessing and at
the same time are blessed, because "he who can take" takes, and the
one seed comes forth according to the quality of its soil.[45]

This theme of the deceitful entry of evil membership into the heart
of the Church is taken up in Rule V in the image of the double gateways of
Jerusalem, the city of God.

Anderson remarked on the long "digression"[46] relating to the law of
the Sabbath in that section of the *Book of Rules* which Tyconius has called
"Of Times"; but it is arguable whether it is a digression. Both implicitly by
the sheer length of the discussion, and explicitly by the introductory comment, the author makes these sections on the Sabbath laws central to his exposition of "times." He introduces the argument concerning the Sabbath in
the context of the interpretation of the "legitimate" number, one thousand:

Several times, one day is 1,000 years just as it is written: "In the
day you taste from the tree you shall surely die"[47] and the first
seven days are seven thousand years: the Lord worked for six days
"and rested from all his works on the seventh day and he blessed and

---

[45]LR 29:2-6. Anderson, *Book of Rules*, 90. Matt 19:12.

[46]Anderson, *Book of Rules,* 168, footnote 76. "At this point
Tyconius broke away from his discussion to an extended allegorical exegesis
of the injunction to observe the sabbath day" (see Exod 20:8-11; Deut 5:12-
5).

[47]Gen 2:17.

sanctified it."[48]   However, the Lord says, "My father is working still."[49] For just as he laboured over this world for six days, so he labors over the spiritual world, which is the Church, for six thousand years, about to cease on the seventh day which he blessed and made eternal.

Then he continues:

That is why, among the rest of his commands, the Lord taught nothing more sharply than that we observe and love the Sabbath day. However, he who does the precepts of God loves the Sabbath of rest. Therefore God warns the people not to enter the gates of Jerusalem with a load on the Sabbath day, and he threatens the gates and one going in and out through them . . . and if you will not hear me so that you will keep the Sabbath day holy, as not to carry loads nor enter the gates of Jerusalem on the Sabbath day then I will kindle a fire in its gates, and it shall consume the routes to Jerusalem and it shall not be extinguished [Jer 17: 27].[50]

Since seven (the Sabbath) is a "legitimate" number, according to Tyconius, this passage is not to be interpreted quantitively, the warnings about the mysterious double gates of Jerusalem being directed at the Church:

It would have sufficed to have briefly commanded that there be no work on the Sabbath; so why did he say, "Do not carry loads

---

[48]Gen 2:2-3.

[49]John 5:17.

[50]LR 61:25 - 62:7; 26-8. Anderson, *Book of Rules,* 166-8.

through the gates of Jerusalem? Or if there was a need to say the type of work, why did he say, "Do not carry through the gates?" For one cannot bring loads into the city through walls and roofs. . .[51]

There are two gateways into Jerusalem. "Jerusalem is bipartite and its gates are bipartite."[52] The lower gates are presided over by the devil and his vicars, "false prophets who are preachers of the law . . . they are hiding, in the highest sense of that word "the keys of the kingdom of heaven."[53] Christ is the holy gate of the city of Jerusalem, and his vicars are the keepers of the law:

> However, if anyone entered through the precepts of those presiding "on the throne of Moses," he enters through Christ . . . for the precepts are his, he unloads the burden of their sins -- and without it enters into the rest of the Sabbath.[54]

Commentators of Rule III have noted the striking image of the law as a walled enclosure, through which there is but one door which opens to life – grace:[55]

---

[51]LR 62:30 - 63:2. See Anderson, *Book of Rules,* 169.

[52]LR 63:3.

[53]LR 63:14.

[54]LR 63:17-20. Anderson, *Book of Rules,* 171.

[55]Babcock, "Augustine and Tyconius," 1213. LR 17:27.

But once the law was given, "the passions which come through the law were at work in our members" [Rom 7:5], forcing us into sin and driving us necessarily toward faith, which would cry out for God's grace to help us endure. We were kept in prison, while the law threatened death and surrounded us with an insurmountable wall wherever we turned. Grace was the one and only door *sola una ianua fuit gratia* in this wall. Faith was the guard in charge of this door, so that no one could escape from the prison unless faith opened the door. Failure to knock at this door meant dying within the walls of the law.[56]

Grace, the one door to life from the "confinements"[57] of the Law, in Rule III, and Christ, the "holy gate of Jerusalem" through which one enters into the "rest of the Sabbath," Rule V, are evocative images which establish a network of relationships between Rule III and Rule V. However, while highlighting the ongoing work of salvation in the Church, the thought of the corresponding forces of death and destruction within the body of the Church is never far from mind. Rule III ends with a reminder of the deceitfulness that characterizes the evil seed, the "sons of the devil creeping in 'to spy out our freedom.'"[58]

---

[56]LR 17:18-26. Froehlich, *Biblical Interpretation,*119.

[57]LR 18:1-4.

[58]LR 30:20, 21 cf. Gal 2:4.

They came "according to the operation of Satan, in all power with false signs and miracles, spiritual beings of wickedness in the heavenly places."[59]

Tyconius concludes his long commentary on the double gates of Jerusalem in Rule V with a final reference to these deceitful brethren:

> Those are the thieves who enter into their Jerusalem, not through the true door but through the door of their own gates, and God will kindle a "fire in the gates of Jerusalem," and it will consume its routes "and it will not be extinguished."[60]

The theme of the "deceitful" presence of evil in the Church is an important indictator of the difference between Tyconius' ecclesiology and that of his fellow Donatists. For the Donatists the Catholics, tainted by "traditor" bishops, were the spiritually "unwashed" since their baptismal waters were "un-vivified" by the Spirit. On the other hand, Tyconius argued that good and evil were found throughout the Church, and it is only through the grace of God that the signs that distinguish who is "separate from Jesus" are revealed.

The Church is not yet drawn "from the midst." It is still a "bipartite" society. The revelation to the sinners in the Church of their perilous condition is a gift of the Spirit to the Church so that those who now find themselves "separate from Jesus" may knock at the door of Grace (LR 17:26).

---

[59] Eph 4:12, (the "heavenly place" for Tyconius is the Church).

[60] LR 63: 28 - 64: 2, Jer 17: 27. Anderson, *Book of Rules,* 172.

4. Rule IV, the central focus of the hermeneutical theory

Rule IV, standing at the center of the seven chapters, is one of the most concentrated and difficult sections of the *Book of Rules*. In the development of the distinctions between "species" and "genus," Tyconius not only argues that both of these prophetic modes are directed at the life of the Church – that is, both are to be interpreted "spiritually" – [61] but it is in this chapter that the significance of the term "spiritual" becomes apparent. Much more is at stake than a simple avoidance of the term "allegorical."[62] Rule IV is central to the development of pneumatology in relation to the ecclesial nature of the task of Christian hermeneutics.

The discussion of the pneumatology of the *Book of Rules* is reserved to Chapter Five, but there are a number of points to note at this stage in connection with the analysis of the structuring of the *Book of Rules*.

First, in arguing that Rule IV is the focus of the *Book of Rules* from the point of view of the elaboration of the hermeneutical theory, it is important to note that it is here that one finds the greatest concentration of technical terms.[63]

Second, Rule IV testifies to Tyconius' own awareness of symmetrical patterns in the prophetic material. He bids the reader of the prophetic text

---

[61]LR 52:4.

[62]cf. Tertullian "On the Resurrection of the Flesh" XX. Tertullian insists on the importance of the literal understanding of "the downfall of nations and cities, of Tyre and Egypt, and Babylon and Edom and the navy of Carthage," and is suspicious of the excessive use of figurative interpretation. "Spiritual" interpretation in Tyconius means more than allegorical language. It is to be understood within the context of the "spiritual" world, that is, the Church. LR 61:31. The meaning of the Tyconian "spiritual" interpretation is explored in Chapter Five.

[63]See Chapter Five.

to take careful note of the intricate "transitions" between "genus" and "species" type prophecy in the text:

> For while it is talking about the species, it passes over into the genus so that the transition may not immediately appear clear, but passing over it adds words which may apply to both, until it may gradually withdraw a measure of the species and the translation be elucidated, since those things which begin from the species would not agree unless in the genus. And in the same way it leaves the genus, returning to the species.[64]

Anderson remarks, in his commentary:

> With his typical brevity, Tyconius has set forth what he considered the basic and most common species-genus arrangement: moving from the *species* to *species and genus* then to *genus,* then either to *genus and species* and back to *species* or directly from *genus* to *species* without the ambiguous transition.[65]

It is interesting to note the symmetrical patterning of the transitions according to Tyconius' reading of the text.

a. *species*

b. *species/genus*

c. *genus*

b' *genus/species*

a' *species*

---

[64]LR 32:5-12. Anderson, *Book of Rules,* 101.

[65]Anderson, *Book of Rules*, 101, footnote 11.

There is no suggestion in Tyconius' argument that this is a rigidly observed pattern; on the contrary, Tyconius suggests alternative transitions. What *is* significant is his awareness of the patterning of the "transitions"[66] from species to genus and so on.

It has been the purpose of this survey of the literary function of recurring images and themes, e.g. the "stones" and "mountains" in Rules I and VII, the "separation" of good and evil members in Rules II and VI, and the "deceitful" presence of evil in the Church in Rules III and V, to argue for a concentric patterning of the material in which the reader's attention would be drawn to the fullest exposition of the hermeneutical scheme in the center of the *Book of Rules*. Rule IV is introduced by an elaborate preamble in which Tyconius disclaims the "rhetorical skill of human wisdom" and claims rather "to be speaking according to the mysteries of divine wisdom by the instruction of the Holy Spirit."[67] The relationship between the pneumatological teaching in Rule IV and that of the "mystical rules" of the Prologue is central to the analysis of the Tyconian hermeneutical theory in Chapter Five of the present work.

THE DOUBLE LITERARY STRUCTURE OF THE BOOK OF RULES

In the previous chapter it was argued that there was a double purpose in the writing of the *Book of Rules;* the first was the explicit purpose, the elaboration of the hermeneutical system, and the second was to address a question central in the disputes between the Catholics and Donatists, the

---

[66]Writing on the structure of the Book of Wisdom, Addison Wright claims: "The use of symmetrical arrangements, announcements of subjects, 'mots crochets' and inclusions is attested in biblical and extra-biblical literature alike." Addison Wright, "The Structure of the Book of Wisdom" *Biblica* 48 (1967): 164.

[67]LR 31:9-13.

"mystery of iniquity" in the Church. The symmetrical structure fits this double intention very well because of the double literary focus of this kind of pattern. The obvious literary focus is Rule IV, the center of the sets of parallel topics, while a second movement is established by the cumulative force of the logic of the argument as it moves from Rule I through to Rule VII, the conclusion of the book.

    (a) the "concentric" argument focused on Rule IV.

    (b) the "linear" argument from Rule I to Rule VII.

In the *Book of Rules*, the static center of the literary structure is Rule IV, in which is concentrated the fullest exposition of the hermeneutical theory, the pneumatological character of biblical hermeneutics.[68] The linear movement from Rule I through Rule VII follows the lines of argumentation concerning the issue that dominated African ecclesiology, the question of evil membership in the Church.

This chapter has studied, first, the parallel features of the topics building up the concentric arrangements around Rule IV. Now the cumulative argument from Rule I through Rule VII will be considered in relationship to Tyconius' theme of the "mystery of iniquity."

While carefully positioning the full development of his theory in the center of the *Book of Rules*, Tyconius uses the linear thrust of the argument to exemplify the urgent pastoral task of the biblical exegete in the Church.

THE LINEAR ARGUMENT (RULE I -VII), "THE MYSTERY OF INIQUITY"

To argue for a thematic development of the argument in the *Book of Rules* from Rule I through Rule VII is to draw attention to the question of

---

[68]See Chapter Five.

the conclusion of the book and in particular to the question of the integrity of
the manuscripts that have survived.

Addressing this question, Monceaux comments:

> Considéré comme œuvre littéraire, dans son aspect extérieur et la
> composition, abstraction faite du fond, le livre n'est pas sans défaut.
> Notons, en passant, qu'il est aujourd'hui un peu incomplet: il se
> termine brusquement sur une citation d'Ezéchiel. Cette lacune finale
> parait assez considérable: il manque, tout au moins, le commentaire
> du verset d'Ezéchiel, et, probablement, une partie importante du livre
> VII qui contenait d'autres exemples avec une conclusion. La lacune,
> évidemment, est le fait d'un copiste ou le résultat d'un accident.[69]

Monceaux suggests that the conclusion of Rule VII, and perhaps an
epilogue, may have been lost.   Burkitt's edition of the *Book of Rules* suggests that Tyconius' conclusion has been lost by placing a series of asterisks
after the last verse. This loss must have been earlier than the ninth-century
Reim's manuscript which leaves the last of the double columns blank.
However, an analysis of the argument from Rule I to Rule VII suggests that
there is a strong case for arguing that the *Book of Rules* is complete as it
has been transmitted.

As it now stands, the final sentence of the *Book of Rules* marks the
conclusion of the last verse of the second of the two exegetical passages
treated in Rule VII; not only is it the formal conclusion in the exegesis, but
the solemn tones of the final passage, "You were made for destruction and
you will cease to be" make for a fitting conclusion to the theme that has

---

[69]Monceaux, *Histoire Littéraire de l'Afrique Chrétienne V*, 81.

threaded its way through the whole work – the "mystery of iniquity" in the "midst" of the Church.[70]

The linear development of this argument is emphasized by explicit references to the theme at the end of each chapter. Positioned at the point of transition between one rule and the next, the theme of the "mystery of iniquity" in the Church is integrated into the argument of the next rule. In this way Tyconius not only achieves the pedagogical and stylistic purpose of alerting the reader to the next stage of the argument, but he deepens this theme as he moves through the frame of the seven rules.

We see this at the end of Rule I where after summing up the argument of the rule of "the Lord and His Body," he introduces the concept of the bipartite Church of Rule II, and warns in terms of 2 Thessalonians of the need for watchfulness for the presence of evil in the midst of the Church.[71]

Rule II concludes that "the one body of the seed of Abraham increases in all things and flourishes and perishes."[72]

Rule III concludes with the further reference to 2 Thessalonians 2, the imminent "departure" which is the "revelation" of "the man of Sin" in the departure of Lot from Sodom.[73]

Rule IV ends in the warning that the fight of the saints is not against human things, "but against spiritual wickedness in heavenly places."[74]

---

[70]2 Thess 2.

[71]LR 8:2.

[72]LR 11:27, 28.

[73]LR 31: 3-5.

[74]LR 54:23, 4, Eph 6:12.

The conclusion of Rule V speaks of the deluge:

> For even the hundred years in which the ark was being constructed is the whole time in which the Church is being constructed, and in that time it governs all those perishing in the flood.[75]

Rule VI concludes with a warning against the deceitful works of the Antichrist, "asserting with signs and wonders" of the inner chamber that these are the works of Christ. The apostle warns them to live by healthy caution, saying, "Little children, keep yourselves from idols."[76]

The last verses of Rule VII carry the same message, a solemn denunciation of the destiny of the evil seed, the "opposing body," that has been the constant theme of the *Book of Rules:* "you were made for destruction and you will cease to be."[77]

In his analysis of the *Book of Rules*, Monceaux had raised the question whether all the rules were really hermeneutical principles or whether some rules were theoretical and others were practical expositions of the theory. He suggested that Rules I, II and VII were theoretical and IV, V and VI, illustrations of the theory.[78]

The present analysis has argued against such an interpretation. All seven rules are properly hermeneutical principles,[79] and they have been so

---

[75]LR 66:6-9. Anderson, *Book of Rules*, 178.

[76]LR 70:9. 1 John 5:1.

[77]LR 85:27.

[78]Monceaux, *Histoire Littéraire de l'Afrique Chrétienne*, 182.

[79]What Tyconius means by "rule" is examined in Chapter Five.

ordered that the full exposition of his general theory of hermeneutics lies at the center of the *Book of Rules* in Rule IV. However, there is a sense in which Tyconius both develops a hermeneutical theory and provides a practical demonstration of his theory. It is not in a division between theoretical and practical "rules," but rather in the double structure of the *Book of Rules* itself.

The symmetrical structure is a vehicle for the elaboration of the hermeneutical system, while in the linear argument from Rule I through to Rule VII, he demonstrates the practical task of the Christian exegete as servant of the Word. The Christian exegete, under grace,[80] and guided by the "logic of the rules," labors that the prophetic word be heard – the word that calls the "sevenfold" Church[81] to fidelity and to conversion.

That the last words of the *Book of Rules* are the words of Scripture, rather than the words of the human interpreter, is a point which is not without significance as we turn to the study of the hermeneutic theory that underlies the *Book of Rules*.

---

[80]LR 4:13 - 15; 31:17, 18.

[81]LR 11:1-5.

CHAPTER FIVE

THE HERMENEUTICAL THEORY

THE MYSTICAL RULES

To come to a better understanding of the hermeneutical theory of the *Book of Rules* one must first ask what is the Tyconian notion of "rule," what does he mean by the "logic of the rules," and even more importantly, in what sense are the rules "mystical."

One of the sharpest criticisms levelled by Augustine at the *Book of Rules* was that Tyconius was raising false hopes in his claim that a mere seven rules could illumine all the obscurities of Scripture.

Hic si dixisset, Sunt enim quaedam regulae mysticae, quae nonnullos Legis recessus obtinent, aut certe, quae Legis magnos recessus obtinent; non autem quod ait, universae Legis recessus: neque dixisset, clausa quaeque patefient, sed, clausa multa patefient; verum dixisset, nec tam elaborato atque utili operi suo plusquam res ipsa postulat dando, in spem falsam lectorem ejus cognitoremque misisset.[1]

Now, if he had said, "There are certain mystical rules which hold the key to some of the secrets of the law" or even "which hold the key to the great secrets of the law" and not what he does say "the secret recesses of the whole law;" and if he had not said, "what is shut

---

[1]Augustine, *De Doctrina Christiana* 82:16-18. PL 34 16-121.

shall be laid open," but, "many things that are shut shall be laid open," he would have said what is true, and he would not, by attributing more than is warranted by the facts of his very elaborate and useful work, have led the reader into false expectations.[2]

Augustine does not doubt that these rules "as expounded by their author, do indeed, when carefully considered, afford considerable assistance in penetrating the secrets of the sacred writings."[3] However, he claims that on a number of occasions, the author solves difficult passages without applying any of these seven rules. Augustine further claims that to draw up a collection of all the problematic passages in Scriptures which would *not* be elucidated by any of the seven rules would be an immensely tedious work.[4]

It is not only that the *Book of Rules* advocates just seven rules that poses a problem for Augustine, but that Tyconius places such value on what he terms "rules" *has velut regulas,*

> Iste autem cum has velut regulas commendaret, tantum eis tribuit, quasi omnia quae in Lege, id est, in divinis Libris obscure posita invenerimus, his bene cognitis atque adhibitis intelligere valeamus.[5]

The author, himself, however, when commending these rules, attributed so much value to them that it would appear as if, when they

---

[2]Augustine, *On Christian Doctrine,* 568.

[3]Augustine, *On Christian Doctrine,* 568.

[4] Augustine, *On Christian Doctrine,* 568.

[5]Augustine, *De Doctrina Christiana,* 82:1-4.

were thoroughly known and duly applied, we should be able to interpret all the obscure passages in the law, that is, the sacred books.[6]

To come to grips with the problem of Tyconius' concept of *regula*, first it is necessary to analyze the preamble to the *Book of Rules*.

ANALYSIS OF THE PROLOGUE OF THE BOOK OF RULES.

a. The skopos

Necessarium duxi ante omnia quae mihi videntur libellum regularem scribere, et secretorum legis veluti claues et luminaria \fabricare.

All things considered I found it necessary to write an essay about the rules and to fabricate so to speak keys and windows appropriate to the secrets of the Law.

b. The proposition

Sunt enim quaedam regulae mysticae
quae universae legis recessus obtinent
et veritatis thesauros aliquibus invisibiles faciunt.

There are certain mystical rules
which withhold the hidden parts of the universal Law
and render invisible for some people the treasures of truth.

c. The logic of the rules

quarum si ratio regularum sine inuidia ut communicamus

---

[6]Augustine, *On Christian Doctrine,* 568.

accepta fuerit

clausa quaeque patefient

et obscura dilucabuntur

Should the logic of these rules be recognized as readily as we communicate it

then anything closed would be opened

and what is dark would be illumined.

d. The telos

ut quis prophetiae inmensam siluam perambulans

his regulis quodam modo lucis tramitibus deductus

ab error defendatur.

so that the one walking on the way through the immense
                         forest of prophecy
guided as it were along paths of light

would be protected against error.

a. Skopos:

The author sets out "to write" a *libellum regularem* [7] and "to make"
keys and windows for the secrets of the Law.

b. The proposition: The rules – their nature and efficiency.

---

[7]LR 1:1, 2 regularem. The Latin authors refer to "libri regulares"
containing rules for guidance. Caelius Aurelius (early fifth century), *Tardae
Passiones* 2, 11, 145. Lewis & Short, *A Latin Dictionary* (Oxford:
Clarendon Press, 1879, 1984), 1553.

The "mystical" nature of the seven rules is stated in the principal clause, "There are certain mystical rules". Their efficiency is described in the two subordinate clauses,

(i) which hold the hidden parts of the universal Law

(ii) which render invisible for some the treasures of truth. These "mystical" rules, as the subjects of the two verbs, "obtinent" and "faciunt," are active principles in the Scripture and in the process of interpretation. First, they *obtinent*, they "hold," "possess," or "retain" *recessus* [8] "recesses" of the whole of the Law. Second, they make the treasures of truth invisible to some, *aliquibus invisibiles*.

One of the remarkable features of Augustine's citation of the Tyconian Prologue, according to the Minge edition, is to be found in this section.

The Prologue in Burkitt's edition of *The Book of Rules:*	The Prologue in Augustine's *De Doctrina Christiana:*
et veritatis thesauros aliquibus *invisibiles* faciunt.	et veritatis thesauros aliquibus *invisibiles visibiles* faciunt.[9]

The Minge text of the *De Doctrina Christiana* adds *visibiles*, which completely changes the meaning of the passage. For Augustine, the mystical rules make *visible* the treasures of truth which are invisible to some; but in Burkitt's edition and the *Monza Epitome*,[10] the mystical rules make the trea-

---

[8]Recessus (accusative plural) a going back, a retreating, a recess, intricacies. Grammatica plus habet in recessu, quam fronte promittit [Quintilian. I. 1, 4].

[9]Augustine *De Doctrina Christiana* III; 82:9, 10.

[10]LR 1:4; "Monza Epitome" 1:4, Burkitt, *Book of Rules,* Appendix I, 89.

sure of truth *invisible* to some. One of the challenges to understanding the nature and efficiency of the "rules" as stated in the Tyconian prologue is precisely that the "rules" actively obscure the meaning of Scripture "for some."

Even a superficial comparison of the hermeneutical "rules" in Augustine's *De Doctrina Christiana* and the "rules" in Tyconius reveal a fundamental difference in concept of *regula* in scriptural interpretation. Augustine brings to the problems and difficulties of scriptural exegesis the literary tools of his own rhetorical background. In other words, for Augustine, hermeneutical rules tend to be *extrinsic* to the text, whereas, for Tyconius, they are *intrinsic* to the text of Scripture. They are "mystical" in that they are discovered in Scripture, and they are active in Scripture.

c. *Ratio regularum* the logic of the rules

Tyconius, having dealt with the *objectivity* of the rules of Scripture, next introduces the *subjective* element of scriptural interpretation – "*if* the logic of the rules be accepted without prejudice as we set them down."

> *quarum si ratio regularum sine inuidia ut communicamus accepta fuerit . . .*

The conditional aspect of hermeneutics is not which rules or how many rules are brought to bear upon the scriptural texts, but whether the logic of the rules *ratio regularum* is accepted. It is the "logic" of the mystical rules which is to be "discerned."

> sola ratio discernit[11]
> ratione discernendum[12]

---

[11]LR 2:2.

[12]LR 3:13; 3:30.

ratione cognoscitur[13]

ista quidem, quamuis hoc quoque Dei gratia sit, adhibita tamen ratione aliquando facilius uidentur[14]

The active response of the interpreter under grace is directed to understanding the logic of the texts which have been "in-formed" by the mystical rules.

If the logic of the rules is accepted, then

clausa quaeque patefient what was shut will be opened

et obscura dilucabuntur, and light will be shed on what was obscured.

What was shut and held secret, what was made invisible by the "mystical rules" in section (b) is now opened and illumined, *if* the logic of the rules is carefully followed.

The carefully balanced imagery of sections (b) and (c) of the prologue is disturbed by the addition of "visible" in Augustine's citation, whereas a careful attention to the structural parallelism is a constant feature of Tyconius' literary style.

d. *The Telos*

The last few lines of the prologue describe the end toward which the whole work is dedicated, that the interpreter be guarded from error.

ut quis prophetiae inmensam siluam perambulans his regulis quodam modo lucis tramitibus deductus ab errore defendatur.

---

[13]LR 3:27.

[14]LR 4:12.

We note again the objectivity of the rules. They are the "givens" of Scripture. In a final juxtaposition of visual imagery, the one walking through the "immense forest of prophecy" is led by the "logic" of these rules as if along "paths of light." The literary artistry of these closing verses is demonstrated by its appropriateness as a kind of finale to a series of images of light and darkness, or of being given access or being closed off, that occur throughout the prologue.

In this well-crafted introduction to his *Book of Rules*, Tyconius indicates that his purpose extends beyond that of resolving problematic passages in the Scriptures. His *Book* presents a theory of hermeneutics, or rather, a theology of hermeneutics. With careful pedagogy, Tyconius introduces his theory of the seven "mystical" rules in the Prologue in a series of evocative images, and then gradually elaborates on this teaching through Rules I, II and III, until he reaches Rule IV, where he reveals the full dimensions of his hermeneutical theory.

As the Spirit is author of "all" the Scriptures (a point insisted upon by the Christian communities since the challenge of Marcion in the second century), then these pneumatological principles are found throughout the Scriptures, *universae Legis/prophetiae inmensam siluam.*[15] It was the very universality of the claims for just seven rules that Augustine found exaggerated and ill-founded. The disagreement underlines the very real difference in the understanding of the nature of "rule" in Augustine's *De Doctrina Christiana* and Tyconius' *Liber*. Augustine brings all the resources of rhetoric to the service of the biblical text, while Tyconius, even when using rhetorical terms like "species" and "genus," refuses a secular connotation of "rule."

---

[15]LR 1:4, 8.

We are speaking now about species and genus, not according to the rhetorical skill of human wisdom, which he who is more able than anyone to speak did not speak "lest he make the cross of Christ empty of meaning," if, like a falsehood, it should need an aid or an ornamentation.[16]

As pneumatological principles, the seven "mystical" rules are present and active in Scripture. They are the "givens" in the hermeneutical process; it is in discerning the "logic" of these mystical principles, under the grace of the Spirit, that the interpreter reaches the goal of truth, or, to change the image, unlocks the treasures of truth, *veritatis thesauros*.[17]

THE "LOGIC" OF THE RULES, RATIO REGULARUM

The concept of *ratio* holds a special place in Tyconian hermeneutics. Rule I begins with the confident assumption that the exercise of simple logic is sufficient to discern the true referent of the biblical text. The sheer force of truth prevents the misinterpretation of the biblical text.

Dominum eiusne corpus, id est Ecclesiam, Scriptura loquatur, sola ratio discernit, dum quid cui conveniat persuadet vel quia tanta est vis veritatis extorquet.

Reason alone discerns whether Scripture is speaking of the Lord or his Body, this is, the Church. It suggests the appropriate reference by convincing argument or constrains the sheer power of truth.[18]

---

[16]LR 31:7-10. Anderson, *Book of Rules*, 98.

[17]LR 1:4.

[18]LR 1:19, 20.

Then, as the argument proceeds, with careful pedagogy, Tyconius begins to suggest that the same rational perception is not always to prove so reliable. He insists that, though the task of interpretation is always under grace, there are times when the interpreter must rely upon God's special assistance.

> Sunt alia in quibus huiusmodi ratio minus claret, eo quod sive in Dominum sive in corpus eius recte conveniat dictum; quam ob rem sola et maiore Dei gratia videri possunt.

> In other cases such reasoning is less successful because the text can be applied correctly to both, either the Lord or his Body. In such instances the proper meaning can be perceived only by an even greater grace from God.[19]

In Rules II and III, he continues to insist upon the need for perceptive awareness of the possible dual reference of the text, and the constant need to follow the guidance of the "mystical" rules in deciding whether the text is speaking of the "right" or "left" side of the Body, or whether the perspective is from that of "promise" or of "law."[20]

Finally in Rule IV he introduces the notion of the vulnerability of the intellect in certain circumstances. The intellect can be distracted from the intended reference by the very complexity of the structure of the text. When

---

[19]LR 4:13-5. Froehlich, *Biblical Interpretation*, 107.

[20]LR 28:23 Lest someone think, however, that the separation of the two peoples is so clear, it was arranged for both to exist in one body, Jacob who was called both "beloved" and "cheater of his brother."

there are multiform narratives "multiformi narratione"[21] the intellect will "insert an impediment" to the perception of the logic of the rules, and so the true referent of the text will be misunderstood.

> . . . quam ob rem Dei gratia in auxilium postulata elaborandum no-
> bis est, et 'Spiritus multiplicis ingressus' legendi eloquiumque
> 'subtile,' quo, dum ad inpedimentum intellectus speciei genus aut
> generi speciem inserit, genus speciesne sit facile videri possit.

> For this reason, the grace of God, whose aid we must ask, must aid
> us, and the "Spirit having entered in multiple ways" for reading and
> of "subtle" eloquence, by which it may be the genus rather than the
> species that can be easily seen, since the intellect will insert for an
> impediment a genus into a species or a species into a genus.[22]

The distractive power of "multiplicity" in drawing the mind from the "simplicity" of truth is a familiar notion in ecclesial literature, and is often imaged as a labyrinth or a dense forest.

Irenaeus concludes a long examination of various Gnostic doctrines:

> After we have, not with violence, burst through the labyrinth of
> heresies, but have unravelled [their intricacies] through merely a
> refutation, or, in other words, by the force of truth, we approach the
> demonstration of truth itself. . . Its definition is constituted after the

---

[21]LR 31:17.

[22]LR 31:17-21. Anderson, *Book of Rules*, 97.

manner in which every true definition is, viz., as simple and un-adorned.[23]

Tertullian concludes an anti-Gnostic treatise with a stinging image.

The doctrines that have grown up among the Valentinians have al-ready extended their rank growths to the woods of the Gnostics. *Atque ita inolescentes doctrinae Valentiniarum in silvas iam exolererunt Gnosticorum.*[24]

In his *Apology*, Tertullian claims that philosophy branched off from the simplicity of truth, (the Scripture), into the by-paths of error.

> . . . the proved antiquity of the divine writings . . . leads men more
> easily to take it in that they are the treasure-sources from which all
> later wisdom has been taken. . . For so, too, if the truth was distin-
> guished by its simplicity, the more, on that account, the fastidious-
> ness of men, too proud to believe, set to altering it so that even
> what they found certain they made uncertain by their adventures.
> Finding a simple revelation of God, they proceeded to dispute about
> Him, not as He had revealed to them, but turned aside to debate His
> properties, His nature, His abode . . . Some of their brood, with
> their opinions, have even adulterated our new-given Christian
> revelation, and corrupted it into a system of philosophical doctrines,

---

[23]Irenaeus, *The Refutation of All the Heresies*, Book X. (The Ante Nicene Fathers, Vol 5; New York: Charles Scribners Sons, 1885), 140.

[24]Tertullian, "Against the Valentinians," trans. A. Roberts, *Latin Christianity*, 520.

and from the one path have struck off many and inexplicable by-roads.[25]

The image of the labyrinth is also found in classical works, as in the *Platonic Dialogues,* where Socrates exposes the verbal trickery of Euthydemus, and describes him "asking, doubting and twisting around the same question like a clever dancer."[26]

Socrates sums up one part of the discussion on happiness:

> . . . We came to the art of kings, and examined it to see if that provided and manufactured happiness. Then it seemed like falling into a labyrinth; we thought we were at the finish, but our way bent round and we found ourselves as it were back at the beginning, and just as far from that which we were seeking at first.[27]

This theme of the susceptibility of the intellect to crafty reasonings is taken up by Gregory Thaumaturgus in his *Oration Addressed to Origen.* Gregory recalls that Origen encouraged his pupils to read widely in philosophy, rather than be influenced by a particular thinker.

> For a mighty thing and an energetic thing is the discourse of man, and subtle with its sophisms . . . And on the other hand, the mind of man is a thing easily deceived by speech, and very facile in yield-

---

[25]Tertullian, "Apology," trans S. Thelwall, *Latin Christianity,* 51, 52.

[26]Plato "Euthydemus," *Plato: Collected Dialogues,* Edith Hamilton and Huntington Cairns (Bollingen Foundation 71; New York: Pantheon Books, 1961) 390.

[27] *Plato: Collected Dialogues,* 404.

ing its assent . . . to crafty reasonings and judgments which are er-
roneous themselves and which lead into error those who receive
them.[28]

Gregory goes on to describe Origen's careful direction of his students
during their philosophical studies.

> . . . they may be compared to men in a deep, dense and majestic for-
> est, *hosper eks hules batheias kai daseias kai hupseles*, into which
> the traveler enters . . . or again, we might take the similitude of a
> labyrinth, which has but one apparent entrance . . . But, after all,
> there is neither any labyrinth so inextricable and intricate, nor any
> forest so dense and devious, nor any plain or swamp so difficult for
> those to get out of who have once got within it, as is discussion at
> least as one may meet with it in the case of certain philosophers . . .
> and he himself, (Origen) went on with us, preparing the way before
> us, and leading us by the hand on the journey whenever anything
> torturous and unsound and delusive came our way.[29]

While they could turn with confidence to Origen as their guide in
traversing the "forests" and "labyrinths" of the philosophers, for their journey
through the Holy Scriptures, they had need of the highest guidance of all.
For Gregory, while Origen is that "most skilled and most discerning hearer of
God" it is the Spirit who is the Leader and guide through the Scriptures.

---

[28]Gregory, "Oration and Panegyric Addressed to Origen", ed. A.
Cleveland Coxe, *Fathers of the Third Century* (New York: Burr Printing
House, 1886) 34.

[29]Gregory, "Oration," 35.

For the Leader of all men, who inspires God's dear prophets, and suggests all their prophecies and their mystic and heavenly words, has honored this man as He would a friend, and has constituted him an expositor of these same oracles.[30]

It is the Spirit who "opens" and "shuts." It is the same Spirit who gives the "word of inspiration" that explains mysteries.

. . . for there is need of the same power for those who prophesy and those who hear the prophets; and no one can rightly hear a prophet, unless the same Spirit who prophesies bestows on him the capacity of apprehending His words. . . and this principle is expressed indeed in the Holy Scriptures themselves when it is said that only He who shuts opens, and no other whatever;[31] and what is shut is opened when the word of inspiration explains mysteries.[32]

In the Prologue of the *Book of Rules*, Tyconius assigns this "shutting" and "opening" function to the "mystical rules" – *clausa quaeque patefient*. They are "mystical" because they are pneumatological principles. The same Spirit is at once Author of the Scriptures and the one who opens what has been shut in the Scriptures. To understand the "treasures of truth" of the Scriptures is to be "illuminated" by the Holy Spirit:

---

[30]Gregory, "Oration," 36.

[31]Isa 22:22; Rev 3:7.

[32]Gregory, "Oration," 36.

et veritatis thesauros aliquibus invisibles faciunt . . . et obscura dilucibuntur . . .[33]

For Tyconius, as it was for Gregory (and for Origen before him), the interpretation of Scripture is a graced activity; one in which the human understanding is opened to the divine mysteries by the Author of these mysteries, the Holy Spirit. The guidance of the Spirit through the "immense forest of prophecy" will protect the interpreter from straying into wrong paths, and drawing false conclusions. The interpreter must be guided by the *ratio regularum.*

ut quis prophetiae inmensam silvam perambulans his regulis quodam modo lucis tramitibus deductus ab errore defendatur.[34]

HERMENEUTICS AND THE SPIRIT

Tyconius stands within a long-established tradition when he turns to the image of the "immense forest of prophecy" in the closing lines of the prologue. From a literary point of view Tyconius' *inmensam silvam* echoes the sixth book of the *Aeneid* where Aeneas, directed by the prophetess of the Cave of Cumae, is searching for the Golden Bough. In answer to his prayer, two doves lead him through the *silvam immensam* that clothes the slopes of the mountain near the Sibyl's cave.[35]

---

[33]LR 1:4-7.

[34]LR 1:7-9.

[35]Atque haec ipse suo tristi cum corde volutat
Aspectans silvam immensam, et sic forte precatur . . .

Vix ea fatus erat geminae quum forte columbae . . .

In the *Book of Rules*, the traveler walking through that forest of prophecy following the *ratio* of the "mystical" rules will be guarded from going astray *ab errore*, from the maze.[36]

In the *Book of Rules*, *ratio* is vulnerable to a special kind of "multiplicity," not the many and dubious paths of heresy of which both Irenaeus and Tertullian spoke, nor the deliberate craftiness of sophistry. Here in the books[37] of Scriptures ratio needs special guidance because of the deliberate intricacy of the structuring of the text with its "multiformed narration."[38]

In the opening paragraph of Rule IV, Tyconius once more insists upon the need of the interpreter for the assistance of the grace of God in reading the text; quam ob rem Dei gratia in auxilium postulata elaborandum nobis est.[39] The Spirit has "entered" the text, *multiplicis* and *subtile*,[40] and

---

Este duces o, si qua via est, cursumque per auras.
Dirigite in lucos ubi pinguem dives opacat
Ramus humum;
Virgil, *Aeneid* VI: 185-96.

[36]Virgil *Aeneid* 6:27. *inextricabilis error* , the maze of Daedalis carved at the entrance to the cave of Cumae. In Ovid, *Metamorphoses* 8, 161, 167, the mazes of the labyrinth. See also P. Courcelle, *Les Pères de l'Eglise devant les Enfers virgiliens* . Archives D'Histoire Doctrinale et Litteraire du Moyen Age (Paris: J. Vrin, 1955), 11.

[37]"Silvae" was also a term for books among Tyconius' contemporaries. Quintilian *(Institutiones Oratoriae, 10.3.17)* explains it as a rapid draft, such as the occasional poems of Statius' *Silvae*. Gellius refers to various literary genres as "Musarium" and "Silvarum." See *Clement of Alexandria: Seventh Book of the Stromateis*, ed. Hort and Mayor (MacMillan & Co., 1902), xiv.

[38]LR 31:7.

[39]LR 31:17, 18.

[40]LR 31:19.

the very text is "in-formed" by the "unity in multiplicity" that is the very mark of the activity of the Spirit. *Multiplex* is used by both Cicero and Ovid in the sense of "winding," "concealing" and "labyrinthine."[41]

But there is more at stake here than a further demonstration of the vulnerability of the intellect in the face of an intentioned complexity. What is of first importance is the theological perspective of the formation of the Scriptures. The Scriptures bear the imprint of their author, the Holy Spirit, in the very structure of the text. They are "multiple" and at the same time "simple," as the Spirit is "simple" in essence yet "multiple" in activity . . . the one Spirit, the many charisms.

SPIRIT AND WISDOM

To appreciate the pneumatological focus of Tyconius' hermeneutical theory, one must look carefully at the way he brings together citations from the second chapter of the *First Letter to the Corinthians* and from the seventh chapter of the *Book of Wisdom*. It is in the conjunction of these Pauline and Wisdom passages that the outlines of his hermeneutical theory can be most clearly discerned.

His approach to these scriptural passages is not that of "proof-texting," but could be better described as "referential" or "contextual." The sense of his allusions to the Pauline and Wisdom passages depends upon the context in which the texts occur.

Tyconius begins by making careful reference to the Pauline opposition between "human wisdom" and true Wisdom of God (1 Cor 2:1-5).

---

[41]Cicero *De Senectute* 15:52 vitis serpens multiplici lapsu et erratico.

... loquimur non secundum artem rhetoricam humanae sapientiae, quam qui magis omnibus potuit locutus non est, "ne crucem Christi" fecisset "inanem" si auxilio atque ornamento sermonis ut falsitatis indiguisset.

We are speaking not according to the rhetorical skill of human wisdom, which he who is more able to speak did not speak "lest he make the cross of Christ empty of meaning," if, like a falsehood, it should need an aid or ornamentation of the word.[42]

Tyconius disclaims the skills of rhetorics, but employs these same skills throughout the *Book of Rules*! He insists that the interpreter of the Scriptures does not turn to human eloquence for guidance, but to the teacher, beyond all human teachers, the Holy Spirit, *magisterio Spiritus Sancti*:[43]

sed loquimur secundum mysteria caelestis sapientiae magisterio Spiritus Sancti, qui cum veritatis pretium fidem constituerit mysteriis narrauit ...

But we are speaking according to the mysteries of heavenly wisdom by the instruction of the Holy Spirit, who since the prize of truth should constitute the faith, narrated mysteries ...[44]

---

[42]LR 31:7-10, Anderson, *Book of Rules*, 98.

[43]LR 31:13.

[44]LR 31:11-4, Anderson, *Book of Rules*, 98.

1 Corinthians 2:6-16 refers to the wisdom spoken to the "mature" *sophian de laloumen en tois teleiois.*[45] It is significant that Tyconius never distinguishes between those "young" in the faith, and those who are more enlightened (the kind of distinctions familiar in the Alexandrians, Clement and Origen). Tyconius' attention is fixed on the relation between Wisdom and the revelation of the Spirit.

> Yet God has revealed this wisdom to us through the Spirit. The Spirit scrutinizes all matters, even the deep things of God.[46]

It is in the context of these Pauline Wisdom/Spirit passages that Tyconius introduces the Wisdom/Spirit nexus from the seventh chapter of the Book of Wisdom:

> for Wisdom, the artificer of all, taught me.
> For in her is a spirit
> intelligent, holy, unique,
> manifold, *polumeres*, subtle, *lepton*, agile,
> clear, unstained, certain
> not baleful, loving the good, keen,
> unhampered, beneficent, kindly,
> firm, secure, tranquil,
> all-powerful, all seeing,

---

[45] 1 Cor 2:6

[46] 1 Cor 2:10.

and pervading all spirits,

though they be intelligent, pure and very *subtle leptotaton*.[47]

Tyconius singles out two of these attributes of Wisdom to characterize the activity of the Spirit.

quam ob rem Dei gratia in auxilium postulata elaborandum nobis est, et Spiritus multiplicis ingressus legendi eloquiumque subtile. . . [48]

In this "multiform" and "subtle" entry into the very formation of the text, the Spirit has so structured the Scriptures that the true understanding is not to be wrested from the text, but to be received as gift.

He underlines this principle at the beginning of Rule VI:

Among the rules by which the Spirit signified the principle – *legem* – with which the way of light should be guarded *quo luminis via custodiretur* one in particular guards the sign of recapitulation *non nihil custodit recapitulationis sigillum ea subtilitate*; so that the continuation of a narration might be seen more than the recapitulation.[49]

The Spirit, as Author of the Scriptures, is weaving narratives of distracting complexity. The attention of the reader is caught by the multiple

---

[47]Wisdom 7:22-3. *The New Catholic Bible* (Camden, New Jersey: Thomas Nelson, 1971).

[48]LR 31:17-9.

[49]LR 66:11-4. Anderson, *Book of Rules*, 180.

strands so that the true reference – the very meaning of the text – is effectively concealed.

This process of deliberate concealment through the very structure of the text is a key issue in understanding Tyconius' hermeneutical theory. It was a well-known compositional practice of both secular and ecclesiastical writers. Clement of Alexandria, in choosing the title *Stromata*, explains that he has "scattered sparks of the doctrines of the true knowledge dispersed here and there, as we promised,[50] so that it should not be easy for the uninitiated who came across them to discover the holy traditions. . .":

> Now it seems that what are known as "miscellanies" are not to be compared to ornamented parks with rows of ordered plantations to please the eye, but rather to some thickly wooded hill, overgrown with cypresses and planes and bay-tree and ivy, and at the same time planted with appletrees and olives and figs, the cultivation of fruit trees and woodland trees being intentionally mingled together, since the Scripture desires to withdraw from observation on account of those who venture secretly to steal its fruits.[51]

The *Stromata*, as a literary genre, exemplified the deliberate structuring of the text to obscure the author's intention by a seemingly artless mixture of many different topics. The holy writings are "authored" and "meaning-ed" by the Spirit, who guards the "treasures of truth." Clement likens the Scriptures to Mary, mother and virgin. The Scriptures "bring forth

---

[50]Clement of Alexandria, *Stromates IV*, 409.

[51] Clement of Alexandria, *Stromates IV*, 195.

the truth and yet remain virgins, hiding within them the mysteries of the truth."[52]

The reference to Clement does not intend to imply any reliance of Tyconius on this second century Alexandrian writer. Rather it points to the general presuppositions that Christian exegetes shared with interpreters of the sacred texts of the Greco-Roman world.

The paradoxical inaccessibility/accessibility of the sacred text is the characteristic function of the "mystical rules" of Scripture of the Tyconian prologue – they make the "treasures of truth invisible to some." The very text of Scripture becomes, as it were, a "tactical labyrinth," the primary and essential quality of which "is the power to obstruct entry, but also to allow it on proper terms."[53]

Tyconius spells out the "proper terms." It is in being guided by the "logic" of the mystical rules structured into the text by the Spirit, the Author of the Scriptures, that what is "shut shall be opened, and what is obscured will be illuminated."[54]

"INTERPRETING SPIRITUAL THINGS IN SPIRITUAL TERMS" 1 CORINTHIANS 2:13

At the beginning of Rule IV, Tyconius introduces the concept of the "intentioned" obscurity of the biblical text. He cites the opposition between

---

[52]Clement of Alexandria, *Stromates IV,* 165.

[53]W. F. Knight, *Cumean Gates: A Reference of the Sixth Aenid to the Initiation Pattern* (Oxford: Basil Blackwell, 1936), 65. The author investigates the widespread use of "maze" entrances for palaces, tombs, sacred caves, sacred dances, processions, sculptural designs. cf. *Aeneid* 6:27, the maze carved at the entrance to the cave of Cumae.

[54]LR 1:5, 6.

human wisdom and divine Wisdom in the opening chapters of *1 Corinthians*. Just as the second chapter of *2 Thessalonians* encapsulates the theme of the revelation of the "mystery of evil" in the Church which threads its way through the *Book of Rules*,[55] it is to the second chapter of *1 Corinthians* that Tyconius turns to "authorize" his "spiritual" interpretation of the Scriptures – "that spiritual things are to be interpreted in spiritual terms."

(1 COR 2:13)

It is significant that both in theory and in practice, throughout the *Book of Rules*, he insists that Scripture is to be interpreted in scriptural terms – not "human terms." He insists that the rules for interpreting Scripture are "mystical" rules; he insists that even rhetorical terms like "species" and "genus," or "synecdoche" or "recapitulation," are to be interpreted according to the "logic" of the "mystical" rules of divine wisdom; that the *ordo* [56] – the logical sequence – of the text is to be discerned under the grace of the Spirit, the Author of Scripture.

This reliance on the authority of the Scripture is especially notable in his references to the activity of the Spirit. The activity of the Spirit is revealed in Scripture itself. The references to the work of the Spirit in the *Book of Rules* are introduced either by scriptural citation or within the immediate context of scriptural exegesis.

Rule I   4:10   Ecclesiae "autem revelavit Deus per
                                        Spiritum suum" 1 Cor 2:10

---

[55]See Chapter Three.

[56]LR 32:11, 12. haec varietas translationis et ordinis exigit fidem quae gratiam Dei quaerat.

	6:24	. . . qui praedestinatus est filius Dei in virtute secundum Spiritum sanctitatis . . . Rom 1:4
Rule II	10:3-5	. . . ipsi autem contumaces fuerunt et exacerbauerunt Spiritum Sanctum. Isa 63:10.
Rule III	16:22-28	. . . vos autem non estis in carne sed in spiritu, si quidem Spiritus Dei in vobis est. si quis autem Spiritum Christi non habet, hic non est eius. Rom 8:9
	18:30-19:3	idem namque Spiritus cf. 2 Cor 3:12-18; Eph 1:10, 2:17.
	21:9-25	. . . a gloria in gloriam sicut a Domini Spiritu.
	[also 18:30]	2 Cor 3:18.
		. . . littera occidit Spiritus autem vivificat . . . 2 Cor 3:6.
		. . . Habentes autem eundem Spiritum fidei, sicut scriptum est: credidi propter quod locutus sum. 2 Cor 4:13.
	25: 8-13	Spiritus Dei contrasted with spiritum servitutis Rom 8:15.

	30:25	. . . semper Spiritui Sancto restiterunt; Acts 7:51.
Rule IV	31:11,19	magisterio Spiritus Sancti. The Spirit instructs; in the context of 1 Cor 1 and 2. Spirit enters *multiplicis* and *subtile*. Wis 7:22, Sir 1:7. *Spiritus multiplicis ingressus.*
	36:20	. . . et dabo Spiritum meum in vos et vivetis . . . Ezek 37:14.
	52:25	quos Spiritus Sanctus deserverit. Unclean spirits will dwell in men when the Holy Spirit has deserted . . . in context of Isa 14: 22-27.
Rule VI	67:31	Multi pseudoprophetae, prodierunt in hoc mundo. in isto cognoscite Spiritum Dei . . . 1 John 4:1.

In drawing up the principal references to the Spirit in the *Book of Rules* it is not intended to explore Tyconius' general understanding of pneumatology, but, according to the limits of the dissertation, to concentrate on the relationship between pneumatology and his hermeneutical theory. Two themes emerge in the scriptural citations: first, the revelatory function of the Spirit, and second, the dualism between those "who have the Spirit" and those without the Spirit. (Rom 8:9).

The revelatory theme is announced in Rule I in the context of the revealing of the "treasures of truth." "God reveals them through his Spirit" (1 Cor 2:10) to the Church;[57] and is taken up again at the beginning of Rule IV, in the context of the opposition between human and divine wisdom in 1 Corinthians, chapter 1 and 2 and Wisdom 7. The second theme underscores the profound duality of the "opposing bodies," central to the *Book of Rules*. Rule II, LR 10:3-5 speaks of those who in their rebellion "grieve the Holy Spirit" (Isa 63:10; Rule III, LR16:22-28), "not to have the Holy Spirit" is not to belong to Christ (Rom 8:9; Rule III, LR 25:8-13), the Spirit of God is contrasted with the spirit of servitude (Rom 8:15; Rule III, LR 30:25), and concludes with the revelation of "the mystery of iniquity" by those who "always resist the Holy Spirit" (Acts 7:51); Rule IV cites the contrasting references LR 36:20 and 52:25, those "resurrected" through the gift of the Spirit (Ezek 37:14), and those "deserted by the Holy Spirit," in whom unclean spirits dwell (Isa 14:22-27). The final reference in Rule VI, LR 67:30-68:4, contrasts the signs of false spirits "separate from Jesus" and the Spirit of God (1 John 4:1).

The opening paragraph of Rule IV takes up these two themes in terms of the revelatory activity of the Spirit in the Scriptures, and the fundamental opposition between the wisdom of God and the false wisdom of this world in the context of 1 Corinthians, chapters 1 and 2.

It has been argued in Chapter Four of the present work that it is in Rule IV, as the center of the symmetrical structure of the *Book of Rules*, that Tyconius provides the fullest exposition of his hermeneutical theory of the "spiritual" interpretation both in its technical and theological dimensions.

---

[57]LR 18:30-19:3, the unveiling of the Law. 2 Cor 3:12-18.

TYCONIAN HERMENEUTICS AND 1 CORINTHIANS

To understand what is implied by this "spiritual" interpretation it is important to note the close correlation between the themes of the *Book of Rules* and the Pauline teaching in the second chapter of 1 Corinthians, the passage which was cited in the first reference to the Spirit in Rule I,[58] and then taken up again in Rule IV.

(a) 1 Corinthians: 1-5

Paul refuses to depend on human eloquence – Rule IV, LR 31: 8-10. The *Book of Rules* refuses human eloquence in interpreting Scripture.

(b) 1 Corinthians: 6

Paul contrasts the wisdom among the "spiritually mature" and the "wisdom of this age. . .," "of the rulers of this age who are headed for destruction."

In the *Book of Rules* the destruction awaiting the evil members of the Church is a constant theme from Rule I, LR 7:27 to the conclusion of Rule VII, LR 85:27.

(c) 1 Corinthians 7-12

Paul speaks of God's wisdom: a mysterious, a hidden wisdom, known to none of "the rulers of this age." It is a "wisdom" revealed through the Spirit.

This point is crucial in understanding Tyconius' insistence on the "hiddenness" of God's wisdom. It concerns "spiritual" blindness. Those opposed to God, "the rulers of this age," cannot comprehend the "treasures of truth" in the Scriptures. The treasures of truth are shut to those "who are separate from Jesus," "who do not have the Spirit." "No one knows the

---

[58]LR 4:10; 1 Cor 2:10.

depths of God but the Spirit of God" (1 Cor 2:11). "The Spirit we have received is not the world's spirit but God's spirit helping us to recognize the gifts he has given us" (1 Cor 2:12).

The Spirit's active assistance in interpreting Scripture is introduced in the *Book of Rules* in reference to these Corinthian passages:

> Having made covenants with the fathers in order that he might be known, God opens invisible treasures to the Body of Christ, treasures which "eye has not seen or ear heard, nor have they entered into the human heart" (1 Cor 2:9)....
>
> quod oculus non vidit nec auris audivit nec in cor hominis ascendit, sed obdurati hominis qui non est in corpore Christi
>
> this, of course, is said of a hardened person who is not in the Body of Christ.[59] To the Church "God reveals them through his Spirit" (1 Cor 2:10). Nevertheless, the use of reason sometimes helps to perceive these treasures more easily even though the perception occurs through the grace of God. quamuis hoc quoque Dei gratia est.[60]

(d) 1 Corinthians 2:13

"We speak of these not in words of human wisdom but in words taught by the Spirit." In the opening paragraphs of Rule IV, Tyconius insists upon the "instruction of the Spirit." *magisterio Spiritus Sancti* (LR

---

[59]LR 4:6-9.

[60]LR 4:11, 12.

31:11, 12). Paul adds "thus interpreting spiritual things in spiritual terms." *pneumatikois pneumatika sugkrinontes.*

I would argue that this verse from Paul's first Letter to the Corinthians holds the key to determining the meaning of "spiritual" interpretation in Tyconian hermeneutics.

THE SPIRITUAL INTERPRETATION OF SCRIPTURE

Tyconius does not use the term "spiritual" until the second half of Rule IV, and it is only after a concentrated use of the "typological" terminology familiar to his African readers that he begins to introduce the terms, *spiritaliter* and *spiritalis.*[61]

Typology represented by the term, *figura,* occurs five times[62] between Rule IV, LR 32:6 and 41:22, principally in discussing the species/genus reference of passages from Ezekiel.[63] Tyconius claims that "all the cities or provinces of Israel and of the Gentiles, which Scripture speaks about, or in which it refers to some act, are a type of the Church," *figuram esse Ecclesiae.*[64]

It is in the context of Ezekiel 21:1-8, that Tyconius first introduces the term *spiritaliter* in the prophecy directed against Jerusalem and its sanctuary which, according to Tyconius, are to be "cast down, demolished and spiritually consumed" *"demolita atque spiritaliter exusta."*[65]

---

[61]P. Bright, "The Spiritual World which is the Church: Hermeneutical Theory in the *Book of Rules* of Tyconius" (*Studia Patristica XXII forthcoming*).

[62]LR 32:16; 33:29; 39:16; 39:27; 41:22.

[63]Ezek 37:21-8; 20:31-8; 36:5-10; 37:11-4.

[64]LR 39:27, 28. Anderson, *Book of Rules,* 117, also LR 41:22.

[65]LR 41:18.

The term, *spiritaliter*, in the context of prophetic denunciation, is used eight times.

(1) Rule IV, LR 41:18. *spiritaliter exusta* – Jerusalem consumed spiritually. Ezek 21:1-8.

(2) Rule IV, LR 48:6. *spiritaliter mortuos* – the citizens of Tyre spiritually dead. Isa 24: 6.

(3) Rule IV, LR 48:22. *spiritaliter cruciatibus* – ...killed spiritually by torments. Zech 14: 11-16.

(4) Rule IV, LR 50:8. *Quae vocatur spiritaliter Sodoma et Aegyptus* (Rev 11:8) – that which spiritually is called Sodom and Egypt.

(5) Rule IV, LR 51:6 *ex quo spiritaliter interficitur mundus* – (the day of the Lord) in which the world is killed spiritually. Isa 13:2-18.

(6) Rule IV, LR 52:4. *Omnia spiritaliter* "Everything, spiritually." – The dashing of "little ones" against the rock is to be interpreted "spiritually." Ps 137:9.

(7) Rule V, LR 64:20. *quod nunc spiritaliter geritur* – the darkness – which is now produced spiritually. Exod 10:23.

(8) Rule V, LR 65:12, 13. *quo tempore invalescit carnaliter eodem deficit spiritaliter* – (the forty days of the flood) "it increases carnally; it decreases spiritually." Gen 7:17-8:13.

His citation of Rev 11:8 is important for understanding the use of the adverb *spiritaliter* in the *Book of Rules*. First, Tyconius invokes the authority of Scripture to advocate the use of this term in a system of hermeneutics for his African contemporaries (but only after a copious use of the more traditional term "figura"). Second, the term *spiritaliter* is used exclusively in the context of prophetic admonitions and denunciations. For Tyconius this usage has both (a) technical and (b) theological implications.

(a) that the passage is not to be interpreted literally.[66]

(b) that it is addressed to a present situation of the presence of evil in the Church.

This adverbial usage coincides with that of *pneumatikos* in the New Testament (1 Cor 2:13, 14 and Rev 11:8).

Tyconius uses the adjective *spiritalis* in more positive contexts – again reflecting the New Testament usage of *pneumatikos* "caused or filled with the Spirit" (1 Cor 2:15; 1 Cor 15:47). In the *Book of Rules,* it immediately refers to the Church in a positive sense.

Rule IV, LR 51:25. *Ecclesiae quae spiritali fruitur vita* – the Church which delights in the spiritual life.

Rule V, LR 61: 31. *ita mundum spiritalem, qui est Ecclesia.* – ("My father is working still" John 5:17). . . . "For just as he labored over this world for six days, so he labors over the "spiritual world which is the Church," for six thousand years .

---

[66]He consistently rejects any kind of millenarian expectations of either rewards or punishments.

An analysis of the use of *spiritaliter, spiritalis* in the *Book of Rules* Rules IV and V suggests that neither as a technical term nor as a hermeneutical method is it meant to supersede typology. Typology remains an essential element in Tyconian hermeneutics. Places, events, persons are "types" pointing forward to the Church. Tyconius does not contest the importance of typology, but claims that all prophetic utterances are first and foremost ecclesiological. All is to be interpreted "spiritually" *omnia spiritaliter*.[67] Throughout the Scriptures, the Spirit, the Author of Scripture, reveals to the Church its nature and its destiny. The Spirit speaks "spiritually" *spiritaliter* to "the spiritual world" *mundum spiritalem*, the Church.[68]

That the Scriptures are addressed to the whole Church is the central contention of the Tyconian system. The word of Scripture is a word of encouragement to the faithful and a word of warning to the sinner. The work of the exegete, under the guidance of the Spirit, is to be a servant of that word which builds faith[69] and which draws to repentance.[70] Toward the end of the argument of Rule II, which speaks of the mystery of the bipartite Church, Tyconius refers to the message addressed to the seven "angels" in Revelation 1:20-3:22. As one of the "legitimate" or "fixed" numbers,[71] seven indicates completeness and so designates the whole Church *hoc mysterio Dominus in Apocalypsi septem angelos dicit, id est Ecclesiam septiformem*. The message of Scripture is addressed to the whole Church, to the saints and keepers

---

[67]LR 52:3.

[68]LR 61:31.

[69]LR 31:12.

[70]LR 11:5.

[71]LR 55:2.

of the precepts *nunc santos et praeceptorum custodes*; and to those guilty of numerous sins and who need to repent *nunc eosdem multorum criminum reos et paenitentia dignos ostendit.*[72]

THE SPECIAL CHARACTER OF TYCONIAN HERMENEUTICS

There are three facets of Tyconian exegetical theory which make the *Book of Rules* an original contribution to Christian hermeneutics:

1. his exclusively ecclesiological understanding of "spiritual" interpretation of Scripture;

2. his theory of the "seven mystical rules" of Scripture;

3. his theology of the Spirit linking his ecclesiology and his hermeneutics.

1. The "spiritual" interpretation of prophecy

In commenting on Tyconius' method of hermeneutics, Gennadius noted that the whole of the Donatist's commentary on the Apocalypse was interpreted "spiritually." The question is in what sense was this "spiritual" interpretation different from that of the Alexandrians and how was it related to the North African tradition.

There is no reference in the *Book of Rules* to the duality of letter and spirit in the Scriptures. This is all the more remarkable when one recalls that Augustine had suggested that Rule III, "On the Promises and the Law," should be renamed the "Letter and the Spirit"![73] Throughout the *Book of Rules* there is no notion of a literal, historical sense of the text as juxtaposed to a spiritual sense. Tyconius does not deny the historical realities of certain

---

[72]LR 11:1-5.

[73]Augustine, *De Doctrina Christiana* III:46.

events in the Scriptures, that certain cities were attacked or destroyed as the prophecies warned, but he maintains that the Scriptures hold mysteries of divine revelation for the Church which are to be interpreted "spiritually." The prophetic admonitions are to be interpreted "spiritually" because this is the time of either the "invisible" growth or of the "invisible destruction" of the Church.[74] The full clear manifestation is reserved for the second advent of Christ. "Now" is the time when the mysteries of God are revealed under the grace of the Spirit. "Then" will be the time of the final manifestation of those who are "separate from Jesus."

This hermeneutical principle is of special significance for the understanding of Tyconian ecclesiology. Ratzinger points out that this is the very point where Tyconius differs from Augustine. While Augustine speaks of the distinction between a visible Church and an invisible Church of the saints, Ratzinger claims that Tyconius is not concerned with the concrete reality of the Church, but with the "invisible" character of its unity, through its bipartite nature throughout the world. Ratzinger further concludes that Tyconius' lack of attention to the concrete reality of the Church as a visible society was connected with Tyconius' own life-situation as a lay theologian and as one at odds with the bishop of his own communion.[75]

Ratzinger's distinction between the ecclesiology of Augustine and that of Tyconius is very important, but his analysis of Tyconius' ecclesiology is problematic. The question of the distinction between a visible and invisible Church is Augustinian rather than Tyconian. Tyconius does not

---

[74]LR 4:22.

[75]Joseph Ratzinger, "Beobachtungen zum Kirchenbegriff des Tyconius im *Liber regularum*," *Revue des Études Augustiniennes* 2 (1956) 174.

speak of an invisible Church; rather he speaks of the "invisible glory" of its coming and its growth in Baptism.[76] Because the mystery of the union of Christ and the Church, the prophetic texts that refer to the glorious coming of the Son of Man at the end of time can, in certain circumstances, refer to the invisible glory of the "coming" or "growth" of the Church. Rule I of the *Book of Rules* addresses this very question.[77]

The distinction Tyconius makes between the visibility of the second coming of Christ and the invisibility of the "coming" of the Church is directly linked with his hermeneutical theory. The prophecies that speak of the cataclysmic disasters of the End Times are actually fulfilled "spiritually" now "in Africa" – "and the end is not yet."[78] The *visible* separation of the two parts of the Church will take place at the second coming; the *invisible* separation is a present reality in the bipartite Church. There are those "in the Spirit" and those "separate from Jesus";[79] those under the grace of Promise and those under the Law.

2. The "mystical rules"

The "spiritual" interpretation of Scripture which Tyconius advocates in his *Book of Rules* is a witness to the special interests of the Christian communities in Roman Africa in the question of evil membership in the Church. This debate had been the cause of intense friction and even schism in the Carthaginian Church between Montanist and Catholic at the time of

---

[76]LR 4:22.

[77]LR 4:22.

[78]LR 67:11.

[79]LR 69:1-24.

Tertullian, in the Decian persecution of the mid-third century between Cypriane and Novatian, and again even more dramatically after the Great Persecution at the turn of the fourth century, this time between Donatist and Catholic.

The seven "mystical rules" whose nature and function are described in the *Book of Rules* are directly related to the preoccupations of the African Church. The *Book of Rules* does not take sides in the contemporary debate between the Donatist bishop, Parmenian, and the Catholic, Optatus, concerning which communion possessed the "marks" of the true Church.[80] Tyconius focuses the attention of the reader on the way in which the Spirit reveals the nature and the destiny of the Church "through all the Scriptures" and in this way makes his own contribution, both as a theologian and an exegete, to the debate on the mystery of evil in the Church.

3. *Pneumatological hermeneutics*

The *Book of Rules* was written about the same time as the Council of Constantinople, 381, in which the divinity of the Spirit was defended by the Council Fathers. While there is at least one reference in the *Book of Rules* to the kind of Christological argument in the Arian debate of the fourth century,[81] there is no indication of the contemporary debate on the Spirit, especially on the ontological level. Here, Tyconius seems an isolated figure, his pneumatology more directly rooted in its Pauline sources.

---

[80]The debate between Parmenian and Optatus is discussed in Chapter Six of this study.

[81]LR 7:4, 5. "Our Lord, because he is God and co-equal with the Father..."

Pauline thought holds an eminent place in the *Book of Rules* and Paul as *the* apostle is a special authority.[82] The present research has already discussed the key role of certain Pauline passages in the *Book of Rules*, - 1 Corinthians:2, 2 Thessalonians:2, and especially Romans and Galatians for the whole understanding of his hermeneutical theory. Pauline pneumatology which so emphasizes the union of Christ and the Spirit is particularly significant for understanding the nature of Tyconian pneumatology. For Tyconius, to be "without the Spirit" is to be "separate from Jesus."[83]

Pneumatological hermeneutics marks the special character of the Tyconian system of scriptural interpretation. The "mystical rules" are to be found through all the Scriptures, and through all the prophecies of the Old and the New Testament because the same Spirit is present and active in all the Scriptures. In the same way pneumatological ecclesiology marks the special character of Tyconius' theology. The people of the Promise who lived before Christ are one with the people of the Promise of the New Covenant because they share the same Spirit.

> Those Israelites who were righteous by virtue of faith had already been called to the same faith. For the Spirit, the faith, and the grace given by Christ have always been the same.[84]

The pneumatological character of Tyconian hermeneutics and Tyconian ecclesiology make the *Book of Rules* much more than an attempt to bring order into the "hap-hazard" and unsystematized state of North African

---

[82]LR 6:1, 7.; LR 31:6, 7.

[83]LR 69:1-24.

[84]LR 18:30- 19:1.

biblical interpretation, as Burkitt suggested.[85] Tyconius has a very orderly approach to his task, as his style of authorship attests; but his hermeneutical theory is at base a theological system centering upon the presence and the activity of the Spirit in the Church. As such it has a claim to the respect and the attention of both systematic theologians and exegetes beyond his own times.

---

[85]Burkitt, *Book of Rules*, vii.

CHAPTER SIX

TYCONIUS AND HIS LATIN CONTEMPORARIES

THE SHIFT IN HERMENEUTICAL PERSPECTIVE

At the end of the fifth century, at least a hundred years after the *Book of Rules* was written, Gennadius included an account of Tyconius in his *Lives of Illustrious Men*.[1] Gennadius places this account immediately after that of Rufinus whom he commends for opening the Latin-speaking Church to the writings of the Greeks. After naming and commenting on the works of Tyconius, Gennadius concludes, "This man flourished at the same period with the above mentioned Rufinus during the reign of Theodosius and his sons."[2]

This enigmatic linking of Rufinus and Tyconius may be explained by nothing more than chronological considerations; but whatever Gennadius' intention, this linkage is not without significance for appreciating the innovatory character of the hermeneutical principles enunciated in the *Book of Rules* for the African Church in the intellectual ferment of the second half of the fourth century.[3]

---

[1]Gennadius, *Lives of Illustrious Men*, 69.

[2]Gennadius, *Lives of Illustrious Men*, 389.

[3]Gennadius belonged to the Semi-Pelagian group in Southern Gaul. Not only was he an admirer of Cassian in whose circle Tyconius' works had been valued, but Gennadius himself wrote treatises on Apocalyptic themes. For Cassian, see P. Cazier "Cassien auteur présumé de l'epitomé des Règles de Tyconius" *Revue des Études Augustiniennes* XXI (1975): 262-97.

Scholars have long agreed on the importance of Tyconius' contribution in turning the tide in the Western Church from earlier millenarian interpretations of the Book of the Apocalypse to a "spiritualized" interpretation which focuses on the life of the Church. "He also expounded the apocalypse of John entire, regarding nothing in it in a carnal sense, but all in a spiritual sense."

It is worth quoting Gennadius more extensively at this point because, though he is referring to the *Apocalypse Commentary*, the same interpretation of the "first resurrection," as occurring "spiritually" in baptism, is to be found in the *Book of Rules*.[4]

> In this exposition [the apocalypse] . . . he doubts that there will be a reign of the righteous on the earth for a thousand years after the resurrection, so that there will be two resurrections of the dead in the flesh, one of the righteous and the other of the unrighteous, but maintains that there will be one simultaneous resurrection of all . . . He makes such distinctions to be sure, between the two resurrections as to make the first, which he calls the apocalypse of the righteous, to take place in the growth of the Church, where, justified by faith, they are raised from the dead bodies of their sins through baptism to the service of eternal life, but the second, the general resurrection of all men in the flesh.[5]

This exegetical focus on the life of the Church was typical of the African tradition but what was a significant departure from tradition was Ty-

---

[4]LR 36:23.

[5]Gennadius, *Lives of Illustrious Men*, 389.

conius' advocacy of the "spiritual" interpretation of Scripture. From its second and third century encounters with Gnosticism, with Tertullian as its spokesman, the Latin Church had repudiated the Gnostic cosmologies and soteriologies, and their "spiritualized" readings of both Old and New Testament Texts. Tertullian, while approving and endorsing typology,[6] insisted upon the obvious and common-sense understanding of the text of Scripture in the light of the "rule of faith": "It is a sign of heresy to find allegories, parables and enigmas everywhere."[7]

The *Book of Rules* is the first witness to the systematic exposition of the theories of "spiritual" interpretation in the North African Church. While the dissemination of his ideas through Augustine, Jerome, Cassian, Cassiodorius, Isidore of Seville and on through the medieval period was to give the Donatist thinker a key role in rehabilitating the spiritual interpretation of the Scriptures in the Latin Church, the present concern is not on the subsequent influence of his ideas, but on the hermeneutical system itself, as it is elaborated in the *Book of Rules,* in which this methodological shift is integrated with the fourth century concerns of the African communities, traditionally focused as they were on questions of ecclesiology and eschatology.

To appreciate the originality of Tyconius, it is important to consider the milieu in which he wrote. This includes not only the Donatist community of the second half of the fourth century (styled by Frend "The Age of Parmenian"[8]), but also the Latin Church beyond Africa.

---

[6]Tertullian, *De Baptismo* 8:11. The ark, the type of the Church.

[7]Tertullian, *Scorpio* 11:4.

[8]Frend, *The Donatist Church,* 193.

If one considers only his own Donatist Church, then in his hermeneutical method and in the literary genres in which he wrote, his is indeed an original genius. He was not only the first to write a systematic work like the *Book of Rules,* but he was the first to write a biblical commentary in Africa. However, in assessing the originality of the Donatist writer it is important to consider the intellectual ferment in the Latin-speaking Churches. Bardy makes the following observation.

> We have reached a period when the cultured classes, after long delays, decided to enter the Church. They brought with them their education, their knowledge and their curiosity, and thus, for a time, even in the midst of the first barbarian invasions, there arose such a blossoming of intellectual life as it is beyond the historian's power to analyze in detail.[9]

Among the innovations were the introduction of Alexandrian methods of exegesis, through Hilary and then through Ambrose, as well as the writing of biblical commentaries, a genre long practiced among the Greek theologians.[10]

These developments in the rest of the Latin Churches raise the question of Tyconius' originality and of the intellectual isolation of the Donatist

---

[9]G. Bardy, *The Christian Latin Literature of the First Six Centuries* (Catholic Library of Religious Knowledge, trans. Mother M. Reginald OP; London: Sand & Co., 1930) 118.

[10]Greek commentaries on the books of Scripture were first written in the third century. Origen wrote many commentaries, e.g., on the Gospels, the Epistle to the Romans, the Song of Songs, the Book of Revelation. Dionysius of Alexandria also wrote a *Commentary on Revelation.* Hippolytus wrote a *Commentary on Daniel.*

community.[11] Were there points of contact between the wider Latin community and the Donatist schismatics? What of Tyconius himself? Did he travel? What literature was available for him? Monceaux suggests he knew Greek, a point that is not without significance for the possible influences upon Tyconius' thought.[12]

Apart from the brief notice in Gennadius, we know so little of Tyconius.

Tyconius, an African by nationality, was, it is said, sufficiently learned in sacred literature, not wholly unacquainted with secular literature and zealous in ecclesiastical affairs.[13]

Gennadius gives the titles of four books. Two works now lost were on polemical subjects typical of the Donatist Church, *The Intestine War* and *Expositiones diversarum causarum*. The other two were more directly exegetical, *The Book of Rules* and the *Commentary on the Apocalypse*.

According to Augustine,[14] Tyconius was excommunicated by Parmenian, the Donatist bishop of Carthage because of his challenges to Do-

---

[11]Both Burkitt (*Book of Rules*, xii), and Monceaux (*Histoire Littéraire de l'Afrique Chrétienne* 165), insist on this.

[12]Monceaux, *Histoire Littéraire de l'Afrique Chrétienne*, 196; C'est donc ce texte latin, traditionnel en Afrique et presque officiel dans les Eglises locales, que Tyconius a pris pour base de son Commentaire. Cependant, l'exégète donatiste ne jugeait pas cette traduction satisfaisante sur tous les points: aussi la contrôlait-il en produisant les leçons d'une autre version. En comparant le texte latin traditionnel au texte grec, il avait constaté des divergences, des inexactitudes, des variantes.

[13]Gennadius, *Lives of Illustrious Men,* 389.

[14]Augustine, *Letter* 93.

natist ecclesiology. We hear no more of his activities after the early 390's, when his works were being earnestly pursued by the Catholic party.[15] Beyond these spare details the rest is speculation.

Methodologically, any investigation into the possible contacts between the thought of Tyconius and his Latin contemporaries beyond Africa will depend on the literary evidence. This presents special difficulties because Tyconius makes no reference to other authors, not even those of his own North African tradition.

To attempt to trace these possible literary points of contact with his Latin contemporaries, it is important to consider the situation of the Donatist Church during the times when he flourished.

THE AGE OF PARMENIAN

For the Christian Church, the middle years of the fourth century may be characterized as "An Age of the Exiles," the exiles being the great bishops whose leadership and literary output were to shape the Church for succeeding generations.

In the aftermath of the Council of Milan in 355, Hilary of Poitiers, Dionysius of Milan, Eusebius of Vercelli and Lucifer of Cagliari were exiled to the East. The Arian George of Cappadocia claimed the see of Alexandria in 356 and Athanasius began his third exile. George had ordained Auxentius, later the Arian bishop of Milan. Thus the Arian debate began to enter the theological consciousness of the West for the first time.

The exiles occasioned a flurry of literary activity. While the exiled Lucifer of Cagliari inveighed against his detractors,[16] Hilary and Eusebius

---

[15]Augustine, *Letters* 41, 42.

[16]Bardy, *Christian Latin Literature,* 80. Bardy lists some of the titles of Lucifer of Cagliari: "That we should not come to terms with

plunged into the study of the Eastern writers. Eusebius translated the *Commentary on the Psalms* of Eusebius of Caesarea, while Hilary read the works of Origen, studied Arianism at close quarters, and produced his great work *On the Trinity*.

These activities and contacts made the return of these bishops just as significant as their exile. By the mid-sixties the intellectual climate of the Latin-speaking West had been transformed.

The seventies of the century saw the Cappodocians in the East and Ambrose as bishop of Milan in the West. Jerome and Rufinus were embarking on their first works of Latin translations of the Greek Fathers. It is precisely to this period of cross-fertilization of Greek and Latin thought that Gennadius alludes in reference to the time of the literary output of Tyconius.[17]

What was the situation in Donatist Africa? Was the Africa of Cyprian now reduced to a provincial back water? Are we to picture a world-denying apocalyptic community – a holy remnant waiting for the vindication of their fidelity and the imminent consummation of the world? Africa as the last bastion of the Church, ringed by the forces of evil, the signs of the Antichrist manifest as Christian persecuted Christian in the name of Christ?[18]

Heretics, The Apostate kings; No one should judge or condemn the absent; Those who sin against God should not be pardoned; Let us die for the Son of God."

[17]Gennadius, *Lives of Illustrious Men,* 7,18.

[18]Optatus, *The Works of Optatus, Bishop of Mileuis: Against the Donatists* (*Against the Donatists*), trans. O.R. Vassall-Phillips (Longmans and Co.: London, 1917), 93. Optatus quotes Parmenian's attack on the Catholic party which "had battened on bloody morsels, and has been fattened on the blood and flesh of Christians."

The Donatists may have sought to insulate themselves from what they regarded as the apostasy of the rest of the Church, but they were far from being insulated from the upheavals resulting from the patronage of the Church of the Christian emperors. The Donatists shared in the "Age of the Exiles." Donatus himself died in exile, and the third in Donatist succession to the see of Carthage, Parmenian, returned to Carthage by the grace of Julian in 363.[19] This man dominated the theological life of North Africa until his death in 391. His works have not survived but we can glean the main lines of his ecclesiology from his Catholic opponent, Optatus, bishop of Mileuis.

Where is the true Church to be found? It is to be recognized by the Ornaments, the endowments given to it by Christ, its Spouse. Parmenian enumerates six, *cathedra, angelus, spiritus, fons signatus, sigillum* and *umbilicus* (the chair, the bishop, sent by God, the Spirit of adoption in baptism, the baptismal font, and the altar).[20]

In his reply to Parmenian, Optatus with heavy irony expresses his gratitude to the Donatist bishop for describing the endowments of the true Church, which is the Catholic Church.[21] He concludes:

> So, to answer you, we have shown what is heresy and what is schism, and which is the Holy Church, and that of Holy Church there has been constituted a representative *et huius Santae Ecclesiae*

---

[19] Optatus, *Against the Donatists*, 95. "Next as is known to all men, there followed another Emperor, who, in conjunction with you, devised evil plans, and from the servant of God became the tool of the Enemy. His edicts bore him witness that he was an apostate. Yet this was the man whom you entreated to be allowed to return. If you deny that you sent such entreaties, we reply that we have read them."

[20] Optatus, *Against the Donatists*, 64, 5.

[21] Optatus, *Against the Donatists*, 91.

constituta est Persona and that the Catholic Church is the Church which is scattered over the whole world (of which we amongst others are members), and that her Endowments are with her everywhere.[22]

Optatus insists that the true Church is characterized by the marks of unity and Catholicity.

> For Peace in unity joined together the peoples of Africa and of the East, and the rest beyond the sea and this unity itself, through the representation of all its members made the Body of Christ solid. And then [referring to Parmenian's return from Exile] over this, the Devil, whom it always tortures to see Brother living in peace was sorely vexed. . . [23]

As a final blast at the Donatist position, Optatus draws upon the image of the Church, the field of wheat and weeds:

> Accordingly we have consented to receive in unity you who have been drawn [to the Catholic Church] for we are not free either to separate or reject even sinners who have been born with us in the one field [and] have received nourishment from one water, that is the one baptism; Even as the Apostles were not free to separate the tares from the wheat (since separation is impossible without destruction).[24]

---

[22] Optatus, *Against the Donatists*, 86, 7.

[23] Optatus, *Against the Donatists,* 97.

[24] Optatus, *Against the Donatists*, 281.

Optatus entered into the polemic with Parmenian in 366 and his work was reissued in 386. There is little evidence that his views had much impact. Parmenian's reputation and authority was dominant in the greater part of the African Church until his death in 391. Augustine returned to an Africa where for all the Imperial harshness toward the Donatists, the Catholic party was an ineffectual minority.[25]

What is of significance for the study of Tyconius in the debate with Optatus is that Parmenian would be ill-disposed to hear a theologian from his own community arguing for the catholicity of the Church, and the acceptance of the growing together (and therefore non-separation) of "wheat and tares" in the one Church. Did Tyconius read Optatus? There is no evidence that he did so. But it is difficult to dismiss the possibility that at least something of the controversy was known to him in the very years of his own polemics with Parmenian on the issue of the catholicity of the Church.

THE CHURCH BEYOND AFRICA: HILARY AND TYCONIUS

Whether one argues for the influence of Optatus upon the thinking of Tyconius or not, the major puzzle still remains unsolved. Was there any point of contact between this Donatist theologian and the new forms of biblical interpretation coming into vogue in the rest of the Latin-speaking Churches? Could he have read some of the early works of Ambrose, bishop of Milan since 373, works in which Ambrose explores the methods of Philo and of Origen? The dating is problematic,[26] and there is no evidence of

---

[25]Jerome comments in 392 that the Donatists "had gained practically all Africa." Frend, *The Rise of Christianity*, 653.

[26]Ambrose did not begin his scriptural studies until the mid-seventies, the years of Tyconius' maturity as an exegete and theologian.

Ambrose's being read in Africa in the seventies or early eighties. But Augustine has preserved an interesting detail in one of his letters, of the works of Hilary being read – and quoted against the Catholics – by the Donatists of his time.

In *Letter* 93, Augustine angrily rejects the Donatist citations from the works of Hilary to prove the corruption of the Churches beyond Africa.

> Such was the time of which Hilary wrote whose work you thought to use as a snare for so many divine proofs, as if the Church had perished from the earth . . . Thus you do injury to a learned man who was earnestly rebuking the slothful and the timid of whom he was in labor again until Christ should be formed in them (Gal 4: 17).[27]

The reference is to Hilary's *De Synodis* where he describes the situation of the Eastern Churches during the years of his exile in the East in the 350's.

> Except for Elensius and a few with him, the ten provinces of Asia, among which I take my stand, for the most part do not truly know God.[28]

It is not surprising that Hilary finds an audience among the Donatists of North Africa, at least in his polemics against imperial persecution from without and heretical bishops within the Church.[29] In a public letter

---

[27]*The Letters of St. Augustine*, 83-139 (The Fathers of the Church, trans. Sister Wilfrid Parsons Washington: C.U.A. Press, 1953), 87.

[28]Augustine, *Letter 93, Letters of St. Augustine*, 87, footnote 108.

[29]Frend, *The Rise of Christianity*, 653.

against Auxentius of Milan, he styles such bishops, not as bishops of Christ but as priests of Antichrist.[30] *Agentes se non ut episcopus Christi, sed antichristi sacerdotes* .

AFFINITIES IN THE WORKS OF HILARY AND TYCONIUS

The themes and arguments of this *Letter* have close affinities, not only with the general lines of Donatist polemics but also with the specific arguments of the *Book of Rules*. Hilary claims that his expulsion from Milan, in spite of his denunciation of Auxentius, is a revelation of the "mystery of iniquity." (2 Thess 2:7).[31]

This theme, so central to Tyconius' thought, is strongly developed throughout Hilary's *Letter* against Auxentius. The time of Antichrist is upon the Church now that it turns to the support of kings rather than to Christ.[32] The forces of evil are enthroned in the midst of the Church, as the Church that suffered persecution now persecutes and exiles bishops. The time of Antichrist disguised as an angel of light has come. The novelties they preach about Christ are the work of Antichrist.[33] Finally, Hilary warns the Milanese against love for the material structures of their Churches in which Antichrist will take his seat,[34] and closes by denouncing Auxentius as a deceiver and an enemy of Christ:

---

[30]Hilary, *Contra Auxentius* 2, PL 10: 609.

[31]Hilary, *hoc mysterium impietatis* PL 10: 615.

[32]Hilary, *Letter to Auxentius* 4. We find the same statement with dramatic overtones in the *Opus Imperfectum in Matthaeum,* an Arian work of the same time.

[33]Hilary, *Letter* 6.

[34]Hilary, *Letter* 12.

Let him assemble against me what synods he will, let him proclaim
me, as he has done already, a heretic by public advertisement, let
him direct, at his will, the wrath of the mighty against me, . . . yet
being an Arian, he shall be nothing less than a Devil in my eyes.
Never will I desire peace except with them who following the doctrine of our Fathers at Nicea, shall make the Arians anathema and
proclaim the true divinity of Christ.[35]

The close following of the themes of 2 Thessalonians 2:3-12 – in
the enthronement of evil in God's temple (verse 5), in the works of deception
and lies, and the revelation of the mystery of iniquity (v. 7, 8) – that we find
in Hilary's *Letter to Auxentius* open up the possibility of contacts between
the thought of the Catholic bishop and that of Tyconius. These themes are
integrated into the very structure of the *Book of Rules*[36] and reflect more
than a decade of imperial repression of the Donatist community prior to the
publication of this work. The confiscation of Church property ordered by the
Proconsul Hesperius in 376 had been the culmination of years of harassment
and turmoil in North Africa.[37] Despite a relative peace for the next twenty
years, the charge of persecutor of fellow Christians was the constant refrain of
the Donatist party against the Catholics. For Tyconius, as it was for Hilary,

---

[35]Hilary, *Letter* 12.

[36]See Chapter Four.

[37]Previous repressions and insurrections occurred under Count
Romanus, 364, and during the revolt of Firmus, 372-5.

this fratricidal hatred instigated by the "princes" enthroned in the midst of the Church was a very indication of the presence of the Antichrist.[38]

Beyond the parallels suggested in Hilary's polemic against the Arian bishop, there are other common features in the work of the two writers. Both Hilary and Tyconius were among the first Latin authors to write scriptural commentaries.

Hilary wrote a number of exegetical works.[39] His *Commentary on Matthew* is the first extant Gospel commentary in the Latin Church; his *Tractatus in Psalmos* and the *Liber Mysteriorum* written after his Eastern exile, clearly reflect his contact with the hermeneutical methods of the Alexandrian Church.[40] Both from the point of view of his contribution to the popularizing of the commentary as a literary genre in the Latin Church, and to the hermeneutical approach found in these commentaries, Hilary's work is significant in assessing the originality of Tyconius' own initiatives in North Africa.

There are many features in these works that make for comparisons with the work of Tyconius. In his *Commentary on Matthew*, written before his exile to the East, Hilary does not follow the Gospel line by line, but turning from the text where the meaning is clear (texts he terms "absolute")

---

[38] See Tyconius, *Book of Rules* Rule VII, etc. Frend suggests that Tyconius wrote his *Commentary on the Apocalypse* in response to the Imperial legislation against the Donatists in the mid-seventies, *The Donatist Church*, 203.

[39] C. Kannengiesser, Hilaire de Poitiers (Saint): *Dictionnaire de Spiritualité* 7 (Paris: Beauchesne, 1968): 466-499.

[40] It is a matter of controversy how much his *Psalms' Commentary* is indebted directly to Origen or indirectly through the Commentary of Eusebius of Caesarea. G. Newlands *Hilary of Poitiers: A Study in Theological Method* (Bern: Peter Lang, 1978), 135.

he concentrates on those sections of the Gospel narrative in which he discovers a hidden spiritual meaning (frequently termed "coelestis significantia").[41] The whole work is developed thematically around dualities such as synagogue and Church; those who deny the divinity of the Son of God and those who do not; and above all the Pauline duality of faith and law.[42]

Specific features of Origenian hermeneutics appear in the *Tractates on the Psalms*. In the Prologue, speaking of the Christocentric nature of psalms, he refers to this referent as the "key" to their interpretation, *clavis scientiae per fidem adventus eius*;[43] while Scripture as a whole has the form of the Incarnate Word, *forma dominici corporis*, in its duality of interpretation – spiritalis/corporalis.[44]

Both Hilary and Tyconius, in their hermeneutical theory, are breaking with a long tradition in Latin interpretation; and it is interesting to note that Hilary, like Tyconius, is very circumspect in his use of the term "allegory," at least, in his first exegetical work, the *Commentary on Matthew*. While it is true that both men challenge the tradition in their emphasis on the "spiritual" interpretation of Scripture, there are significant divergences in method and theory in their works.[45]

---

[41]Newlands, *Hilary of Poitiers*, 22.1, quaestio omnis in absoluto est 15.1, absolute ratio, 56, 59.

[42] Newlands, *Hilary of Poitiers*. See also the dualities, synagogue/church and law/faith in *Tractatus mysteriorum Hilaire de Poitiers traité des mystères*, Sources Chrétiennes par Jean Paul Brisson (Paris: Les Éditions du Cerf, 1947), 150, 4.

[43]Hilary, *Tractus Psalmos*, Prologue, 15.

[44]Hilary, Prologue, 7 Newlands, *Hilary of Poitiers*, 147.

[45]Hilary uses terms such as externa claritas; interioris significantia; coelestis significantia; futura species; futurorum figuratio. These do not occur in the *Book of Rules*.

DIFFERENCES BETWEEN HILARY AND TYCONIUS

Both Hilary and Tyconius share a thematic approach in their exegetical works, and the themes reflect Pauline dualities[46] but their theological focus is very different. Hilary's powerful defense of the divinity of the Son receives scant attention in Tyconius. The African affirms his belief in the divinity of Christ. *Dominus autem noster non est Dei filius praedestinatus (quia Deus est et coaequalis est Patri)* . . .,[47] but his attention is far removed from the anti-Arian polemics of Hilary. His full attention is reserved for the Church, its nature and its destiny.

There is an important difference between the identification of Antichrist in Hilary's *Letter against Auxentius* and the identification of Antichrist in the *Book of Rules*. For Hilary the specific evil is that an Arian bishop "enthroned" in the midst of the Church would be teaching doctrine against the divinity of Christ. It is by no means clear that Tyconius in referring to the "king of Babylon" (Isa 14) and the "prince of Tyre" (Ezek 28) is speaking of Catholic bishops. Such an interpretation would have mollified the ruffled sensibilities of his Donatist bishop, Parmenian, but there is no evidence that such was his intention. In point of fact, his hermeneutic requires a much more subtle presence of the evil "enthroned in the midst" of the Church than Hilary's polemic against the very visible Auxentius "enthroned" in Milan.

The common theme of the Antichrist "in the midst" of the Church, in reference to 2 Thessalonians, *may* suggest possible influence of Hilary

---

[46]Hilary: faith/law; synogague/church. Tyconius: law/promise as well as duality of the Head and Body; and the two "seeds"; the two cities, and the two kindgoms.

[47]LR 7:4, 5.

on the thought of Tyconius, but this is difficult to verify either on external or internal grounds. Such a comparison is more helpful in understanding more precisely certain facets of Tyconian thought.

Aside from differences in theological concerns which reflect the obvious differences between the situations Hilary faced in the middle years of the century in Gaul and Italy, and that of Tyconius in Roman Africa decades later, there are important differences in hermeneutical theory. These differences are critical in appreciating the originality of Tyconius' theory of spiritual interpretation. Where Hilary, in theory at least, accepts the Origenian dualism of the corporeal and spiritual senses, for Tyconius, in a paradoxical unity and multiplicity, the Scriptures bear the impress of the Spirit rather than the dual nature of the Incarnate Word. It is precisely in this centrality of the theology of the Spirit in his *Book of Rules* that Tyconius differs most radically from Hilary in hermeneutical theory.[48]

The attempts to trace the influences of his Latin contemporaries upon Tyconius' thought remain inconclusive. One of the most obvious barriers to tracing the influences that led him to introduce a hermeneutical method so different from that of his fellow Donatists is the very cohesiveness of his thought. His independence stems from the system itself. But while the precise catalyst of his thought remains elusive, an awareness of the milieu in which he wrote is not without value in attempting to assess Tyconius' originality and creativity.

---

[48]Hilary's great work, *On the Trinity*, reflects the Christological concerns of the Arian crisis. It predates the pneumatological debates culminating in the conciliar decrees of 381.

THE ORIGINALITY OF TYCONIUS

The Latin tradition of the fourth century is an amalgam of elements from many different sources. This is revealed in Newland's analysis of Hilary's exegetical work, even before his eastern exile.

> The precise answers to the question of Hilary's sources and the influence of various traditions on the *In Matthaeum* remain unknown. The tradition of Tertullian, Cyprian and Novatian in theology is clearly followed, though at a distance and with considerable independence on Hilary's part. Traces of anti-Arian exegesis are present, though this was not yet the burning issue of the period of the *De Trinitate*. From Tertullian and Novatian and probably other sources, certainly including Neoplatonic influence, came dualist traits, though these may not be exaggerated. Some indirect influence of Origen is likely.[49] Cyprian was of theological importance. The marks of the rhetorical tradition throughout are clear. Hilary may have known Hippolytus' work, though this cannot be proved. The most likely single source of much of the inspiration of his theology of the Heilsgeschichte of the incarnation is Irenaeus: direct evidence for this is however entirely lacking.[50]

An examination of the *Book of Rules* of Tyconius reveals a similar tangled skein of ecclesial traditions. One finds the traditional African themes

---

[49]Newlands, *Hilary of Poitiers*, 98, footnote 85. For a more extensive discussion of Hilary's theological and literary background at the time of the treatise *In Mathaeum*, see Jean Doignon, *Hilaire de Poitiers avant l'Exil* (Paris: Études Augustiniennes, 1971). Doignon excludes even an "indirect" influence of Origen at that early stage of Hilary's theological career.

[50]Newlands, *Hilary of Poitiers*, 98.

inherited from Tertullian and Cyprian: the emphasis on pneumatology, as well as the eschatological elements – the vindication of the persecuted Church, the signs of Antichrist, the expectation of the Second Coming. There are echoes of Novatian's *The Trinity* in Rule I of the *Book of Rules* where Tyconius distinguishes between "unus" and "unum" in the context of John 10:30.[51] Newland's suggestion that Hilary may also have known Hippolytus is also interesting from the point of view of Tyconius, especially in relation to Hippolytus' *Commentary on Daniel* where Hippolytus juxtaposes citations from Daniel, 2 Thessalonians and the Apocalypse.[52]

While the many common elements in the works of Hilary and Tyconius demonstrate their rootedness both in their Christian and in their classic past, at the same time their divergences demonstrate the richness and complexity of Latin thought in the second half of the fourth century. A further element to be considered in the work of the Donatist is that of a North African spirituality distinct from the rest of the Western Church. Frend describes the peculiar features of African Christianity.

In North Africa, Christianity, both Donatist and Catholic, continued the tradition of protest. Views tended to be formulated in terms of

---

[51]LR 7:19-23. cf. Novatian, "The Trinity": 27 *Novatian - The Writings*, trans. Russell De Simone (Washington: Catholic University of America, 1972), 92. John 10:30 "I and the Father are one (unum) . . .He did not say one (unus). For 'one' in the neuter gender denotes harmony of fellowship, not unity of persons."

Tyconius, LR 7:19-23. "Now there is a difference between 'you are one' (unum) and 'you are one person' (unus). When one person is mingled with another in [an act of] will, they are one, as the Lord says: 'I and the Father are one (unum).' When they are also mingled in body, however and are joined into one flesh, the two are one person (unus)."

[52]Hippolytus, "Commentaire sur Daniel" IV, xx-xxi C. Bardy, M. Lefèvre *Sources Chrétienne* 14 (Paris: Les Éditions du Cerf, 1947) 303.

contrast with pagan society. No secular allusions were allowed to appear in Donatist theological tracts. Christianity was regarded as a "law" distinct from secular law. Augustine could take the concept of "Two Cities" as a commonplace among his hearers. Judgment was an all-important influence on him as on his Donatist opponents, and predestination to salvation was familiar to Donatist popular writers two generations before the Pelagian controversy. Sudden conversion through the power of the Spirit was the experience of the Donatist, Petilian of Constantine, as well as of Augustine. Asceticism even, where not connected with the Circumcellions or the Manichees, sometimes took forms more reminiscent of the rule of the covenanters of Qumran than the conventual houses evolving under Ambrose's care in Italy. Much of the harsh edge of North African Christianity was reflected in the concept of baptism and the huge baptisteries that, all over Christian North Africa, symbolized the convert's complete renunciation of the world, its politics, its philosophies, and its literature.[53]

Many of these North African themes appear in the *Book of Rules*. The repudiation of human wisdom,[54] judgment, as well as image, the two cities,[55] and the centrality of baptism[56] are all major themes.

---

[53]Frend, *The Rise of Christianity*, 652, 3.

[54]LR 31:8, 11.

[55]LR 42:6-9, the city of Cain. LR 50:10, LR 72:26-28 Babylon and Jerusalem .

[56]LR 4:29; 36:23; 43:3; 7:6.

On the one hand, the presence of the many elements of African Christianity and of the wider Latin tradition militate against representing Tyconius as an isolated figure either in his own community or even in the wider context of Latin-speaking Christianity.[57]   On the other hand, while these many elements of Latin thought appear in the *Book of Rules,* the independence of Tyconius' arguments and the challenge of his rigorous logic made him an enigma to his contemporaries, both Donatist and Catholic, as Augustine notes:

> Contra Donatistas, inuictissime scripsit, cum fuerit Donatista; et illic inuenitur absurdissim1 Cordis, ubi eos non omni ex parte relinquere uoluit.[58]

> He wrote victoriously against the Donatists and yet he displayed an absurd inconsistency of behavior in refusing to abandon their party altogether.

Monceaux comments on the factors that place him apart from his North African contemporaries.

> Par l'originalité de son œuvre et de son rôle, Tyconius occupe une place à part dans la littérature comme dans l'histoire du donatisme. D'abord, c'était un écrivain laïque: signe distinctif, déjà, dans ce monde si discipliné des schismatiques, où le primat seul parlait au

---

[57]cf. Burkitt, *Book of Rules*, viii. "The work of Tyconius seems to be entirely original; there are hardly any traces of the influence of previous writers in it. But it profoundly influenced succeding Latin writers from the time of S. Augustine onward."

[58]Augustine, *De Doctrina Christiana* III: 30.

nom du parti, et où l'on ne reconnaissait guère aux laïques qu'un
droit, le droit d'obéir. Puis, cet écrivain laïque, plus que personne
autour de lui, avait la mentalité et le tour d'esprit d'un théologien:
aptitude étrange, au milieu de clercs et d'évêques qui vivaient de
traditions ou de préjugés, rééditant toujours les mêmes clichés, et ne
s'intéressant qu'aux querelles d'Eglises ou de personnes. Polémiste,
Tyconius l'était sans doute, comme tout donatiste, et de nature encore plus que d'habitude: mais il l'était à sa manière, qui scandalisait
et irritait les siens, ne cherchant dans la polémique que la vérité,
gardant envers et contre tous son franc parler, sans crainte de déplaire
à ses amis ou de travailler pour ses adversaires, sacrifiant à ses amis
ou   sacrifiant à sa conscience jusqu'à son repos d'homme d'étude.
Cet esprit d'indépendance et de sincérité, il le portait jusque dans la
lecture, l'interprétation et le commentaire des Livres saints: par là,
il réussit à fonder un système original d'exégèse, qui mérita ce priv-
ilège unique, de s'imposer également aux deux Églises rivales, et
d'inspirer Augustin lui-même.[59]

With high praise for this enigmatic figure, Monceaux concludes that
he "recalls Cyprian and announces Augustine."[60] Where he *differed* both
from his Donatist community and the Cyprianic tradition was all too clear to
his bishop, Parmenian. According to Augustine's sources, Tyconius argued
against re-baptism of converts, against the teaching of both Cyprian and the
Donatists,[61] and even worse, he argues against the Donatist self-identifica-

---

[59]Monceaux, *Histoire Littéraire de l'Afrique Chrétienne* V, 165.

[60]Monceaux, *Histoire Littéraire de l'Afrique Chrétienne* V, 214.

[61]Augustine, *Letter* 93.

tion with the true Church, the Church "of the South."[62] The strength of his polemic against the ecclesial interpretations within his own communion is matched by the strength of his argument for a pneumatological foundation for his notion of the Church – or rather his systematic application of pneumatology. This pneumatology distinguishes him from the Catholic Optatus. Tyconius bypasses the whole question of "ornaments and endowments"[63] of the Church, and points to the immediate signs of the presence of the Spirit and union with Christ – the signs of charity.[64]

The pneumatology that underlies his emphasis on the "spiritual" interpretation of Scripture further distinguishes Tyconius from his African contemporaries and also from the earlier millenarian traditions of Tertullian, Irenaeus and Victorinus of Pettau.

THE TYCONIAN SYNTHESIS

It is a comparatively simple matter to say *where* he differs from his contemporaries, but to say *why* he differs is far from simple. Was it merely a dissatisfaction with the general lack of systematic hermeneutics in the Latin Church? Did the application of the "spiritual" interpretation of Scripture result in a radically different ecclesiology and eschatology?

I have argued that the evidence of the literary arrangement of the *Book of Rules* is against fortuitous selection of texts and themes to illustrate his hermeneutical theory. His biblical theory and his ecclesial themes are of a piece. His independence within the Latin tradition (rather than from the Latin tradition) flows from his selection and organization of many of the fa-

---

[62]Cant 1:6

[63]Optatus, *Against the Donatists*, 64.

[64]LR 68:9-13.

miliar themes and concepts into a new synthesis. Like Hilary, Tyconius is distinguished from his contemporaries by his systematic cast of thought. This means that not only is Tyconius the first to propose a coherent system of exegesis in the African Church, he is also the first to propose a focused, systematized theology of the Church.

At the center of Tyconius' theology is the concept of the "bipartite" Church. This is the linchpin of his system. Tyconius takes the eschatological themes familiar to the African Churches – the coming of the Antichrist, the image of the "tares and the wheat" (Matt 13:30) growing together, shadowed by the ominous approach of the Judgment, but he shifts the focus of attention. In the *Book of Rules*, there is a deliberate new focus on the secret presence of the two peoples,[65] the two kingdoms,[66] the two gateways to Jerusalem,[67] the two mountains,[68] and the two cities[69] throughout the Church. The separate destinies of these two peoples are already indicated by the "signs" of being in union of love with Jesus, or the "signs" of being "separate from Jesus."[70]

"Now" *nunc* (LR 67:21) *a modo* (LR 4:16, 24, 26), they are inextricably mixed together like the "tares and the wheat" before the harvest; but "then" *tunc* (LR 67:13, 17, 18, 22, 27), at the coming Judgment,

---

[65]LR 28:23.

[66]LR 75:1.

[67]LR 63:2.

[68]LR 11:20.

[69]LR 42:8; 78:28.

[70]LR 69:16.

Christ's manifestation will reveal their separate destinies.   "Then," those united to Christ will be rescued "from the midst"[71] and united forever with Christ, the Head of the Body.

Just as there was a shift in theological focus from the coming Judgment to the secret presence of these two "peoples," or "orders," in the Church, so too there is a shift from the "then" of the Judgment to the "now" of the Church, and a shift from the apocalyptic intent of comfort and encouragement to a persecuted Church fixing its gaze on the coming Lord to the pastoral urgency of calling *all* the members to the life and resurrection begun in their Baptism.[72] Yet it is far from a Gnostic-type, "realized" eschatology; rather it is a call to repentance, conversion and life in the Spirit in the "now" of the Church rather than in the "then" of an eternal separation from Christ.

The "now" of the Church and the "then" of the Judgment is a continuing theme with a multitude of variations throughout the *Book of Rules* and witnesses both to the vitality and to the disciplined clarity of thought that characterizes the writing of this African systematician.

---

[71]2 Thess 2:7.

[72]LR 43:3; 7:6.

CONCLUSION

The aim of the study has been to understand the purpose and the inner logic of the *Book of Rules*. It has been argued that a lack of recognition of the *thematic* and *systematic* character of the work has made its theory of exegesis as enigmatic to subsequent scholarship as was its theory of the Church to Tyconius' contemporaries, both Donatist and Catholic.

When insufficient attention is paid to the literary clues of parallel images, to literary inclusions or concentric structures, then one is left with the enigma of an author who is so logical in his argumentation, yet so illogical in the overall literary structure of his composition.

When the thematic character of the selection and the commentary of biblical texts throughout the *Book of Rules* is ignored, then the reason for Tyconius' choice of the Book of Revelation as a subject for a biblical commentary remains problematic.[1] On the other hand, if the consistency of the theme of the "revelation" of the "mystery of iniquity" in the *Book of Rules* is recognized, then not only are the thematic links between the *Book of Rules* and the *Apocalypse Commentary* established, but the *Book of Rules* itself may be regarded not as a general introduction to exegesis but specifically as an introduction to the exegesis the Apocalypse, a text which is a veritable "forest of prophecy." This may well have been the intuition of Bede when he

---

[1]K. Steinhauser, *The Apocalypse Commentary of Tyconius,* 251. "Why of all the books of the Bible did Tyconius choose to write a commentary on the Apocalypse?"

prefixed his own *Commentary on the Apocalypse* with a summary of Tyconius' *Book of Rules.*[2]

Even more serious obstacles for the just appreciation of Tyconius' thought are presuppositions about the notion of "rule." Augustine has complained that Tyconius had raised false expectations in claiming that one could be guided through the "forest of prophecy" by a mere seven rules.[3] However, close attention to the grammatical parallels in the preamble of the *Book of Rules* reveals that it is not the rules that guide the interpreter; it is the "logic" of the rules. The rules are not extrinsic rules to be applied in interpretation. The interpreter applies logic, not the "mystical" rules of Scripture.

The seven rules are the "literary" principles that govern the formation of the very text of Scripture. They are those "subtle transitions" in a scriptural narrative by which the Spirit shifts the reference from Head to Body *quando a capite ad corporis transitum facit* (LR 2:14), or from the part to the whole *a parte corporis ad partem....transitus reditusque* (LR 8:8-10)....*dum enim speciem narrat ita in genus transit ut transitus non statim liquido aPareat, sed talia transiens ponit verba quae...*(LR 31:21-23). If the "bipartite" nature of the Church is accepted, then the "logic" of these "transitions" is recognized and the interpreter can walk through the "forest of prophecy" as through "paths of light" (LR 1:5-9).

A further question needs to be addressed. Why *seven* mystical rules? It is too facile to suggest that a "sevenfold" Church (to use Tyconius' term) requires a sevenfold hermeneutical system. The close thematic links between the *Book of Rules* and Tyconius' *Apocalypse Commentary* suggest that it is probable that the *Book of Rules* was intended as a theoretical introduction

---

[2]Burkitt, *The Book of Rules*, xxi.

[3]Augustine, *De Doctrina Christiana* III, 30.

to the *Commentary*. Even more, it may be argued that the two works are so complementary in purpose and subject matter that one cannot be read without the other. While Steinhauser's recent work on the history of the reception and the influence of Tyconius' *Commentary* underlines the difficulty of a complementary study of the two works of Tyconius, at the same time his work provides a methodological guide for such a task.[4]

Even a cursory reading of the *Turin Fragments* of the *Apocalypse Commentary* is illuminating for understanding the terminology and the lines of argumentation in the *Book of Rules*. This is especially true of terms like "recapitulation," which already had a history of technical usage in the African Church before Tyconius. The needed comparison of the use of this term as well as terms like "species" and "genus" in the *Book of Rules* and in the *Apocalypse Commentary* would be indispensable step in establishing any kind of a scholarly consensus about these terms.

While Tyconius' technical vocabulary is still a matter of debate, there has not been a great deal of interest on the question of the number of the rules. Here again it may be suggested that the *Apocalypse Commentary* holds the key to the problem of why Tyconius insists that there are seven mystical rules. A comparison between Tyconius' *Commentary* on the letters to the seven Churches (Rev 2:1-3:22), the seven seals (Rev 6:1-8:1), the seven trumpets (Rev 8:2-11:15), and the seven bowls (Rev 16:1-21) with the argumentation in the *Book of Rules* may well shed light upon the unresolved question of the number of the rules.[5]

---

[4]Steinhauser, "The Tyconian Synopsis," *The Apocalypse Commentary of Tyconius*, 265-316.

[5]C. Kannengiesser, *A Conflict of Christian Hermeneutics in Roman Africa: Tyconius vs. Augustine.* (Center for Hermeneutical Studies. Berkeley, Ca., forthcoming, 1989).

To conclude, then, is no more than to argue for the need for further investigations and even new beginnings of the study of the *Book of Rules*. Chapter Six of the present work drew attention to Tyconius' Latin contemporaries in seeking to consider possible influences upon the thought of the Donatist author, but of equal importance is a consideration of the African tradition that lies behind Tyconius. What of the pneumatology, the eschatology and the ecclesiology of Tertullian, of Cyprian and of the Donatist writers who contributed so richly to the African tradition?   What of the millenarian tradition behind African writers like Victorinus of Pettau and Commodianus which Tyconius refused?

Another whole field of investigation is the classical tradition that lies behind the *Book of Rules*. Of particular importance is the question of the rhetorical background of the hermeneutical theory. The technical vocabulary of Tyconius as well as stylistic devices throughout the *Book of Rules* calls for a careful comparison with the rhetorical studies of Cicero and of Quintillian. A contrasting study of the rhetorical traditions that lie behind Augustine's *On Christian Doctrine* and Tyconius' *Book of Rules* makes for a lively debate.[6]

It has been noted throughout the present study that the style of the *Book of Rules* is at once didactic and exhortative. Tyconius' disclaimer against the "ornaments" of language in Rule IV is itself a rhetorical device as much as a tribute to St. Paul (LR 31:7-10; 1 Cor 1-17). The styles of exhortation appropriate to the speaker and to the occasion are frequently commented on in classic literature. Epictetus argues that oratorical display *epideixis* is not the proper mode for exhortation.

---

[6]Kannengiesser, *A Conflict of Christian Hermeneutics*, forthcoming.

The lecture hall of the philosopher is a hospital; you ought not to walk out of it in pleasure, but in pain. For you are not well when you come in; one man has a dislocated shoulder. . . another a headache. And am I then to sit down and recite you dainty little notions and clever little mottoes? . . . What is the style of exhortation? The ability to show the individual, as well as the crowd, the warring inconsistency in which they are floundering about....[7]

In the *Book of Rules*, the Spirit is the "eloquent" revealer (LR 31:19) of the condition and the destiny of the unrepentant sinner in the Church, as the final words of the *Book of Rules* give grim and ample witness, "You are meant for destruction and you will not be gathered into eternity" (LR 85:27).

It would not be appropriate to the positive values inherent in the *Book of Rules* to conclude this study on such a bleak note. One might ask again what claim can such a work have upon a modern audience. Is it merely a useful gauge to measure the distance between the past and the present of the exegetical task? Methodologically, this is true. Yet the enduring worth of Tyconius' enterprise may be in the very motivation and expertise that he brought to his task of drawing up a system of exegesis that drew upon sophisticated notions of hermeneutics of his time to address what he perceived as immediate questions facing the Christian community.

There is a further challenge at the very heart of the *Book of Rules*. It is the challenge to the Christian Church divided in understanding its very nature. Tyconius refuses to join the sectarian struggle between the Catholic and the Donatist Churches, each claiming to be the "true" Church, each

---

[7]Epictetus, *Discourses*, Abraham Malherbe, *Moral Exhortation: A Greco-Roman Source Book* (Philadelphia: Westminster Press, 1986) 123, 4.

pointing to the "sinful" condition of the other party – the Donatists spurning communion with the Catholics as "traditors" of the Scriptures and persecutors of fellow Christians, the Catholics accusing the Donatists of "rending" the Body of Christ.

Tyconius points rather to that "rending" of the Body which goes beyond institutional and theological controversy. It is a rending of the Body of Christ by that "mystery of iniquity" that separates the sinner from Christ. As one of the significant Pauline commentators of the late fourth century, Tyconius urges all still under the law of sin to go through the "true door," Christ *per ianuam veram* (LR 63:28), into that "spiritual world" where the Spirit vivifies and unites all to Christ (LR 61:31).

Index of Contemporary Authors

Index of Ancient Authors

Index of Biblical References